Another Life

by Derek Walcott

Selected Poems

The Gulf

Dream on Monkey Mountain and Other Plays

Another Life

Another Life

Derek Walcott

FARRAR, STRAUS
AND GIROUX

New York

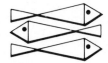

Copyright © 1972, 1973 by Derek Walcott
First printing, 1973
Library of Congress catalog card number: 70-183233
ISBN 0-374-10524-3
Printed in the United States of America
Published simultaneously in Canada by Doubleday Canada Ltd., Toronto
Designed by Pat de Groot

Acknowledgments are made to the editors of *Savacou,*
West Indies, in which sections of Book One were
first published; and to *The New Yorker,* in which
"The Muse of History at Rampanalgas," a
section of Part Four, originally appeared

for Margaret

On the day when I finally fasten my hands upon its
wrinkled stem and pull with irresistible power, when
my memories are quiet and strong, and I can finally
translate them into words, then I shall perceive
the unique and essential quality of this place.
The innumerable petty miseries, the manifold beauties
eclipsed by the painful necessity of combat and
birth, these will be no more than the network of
down-growing branches of a banyan tree, winding
about the sea.

Edouard Glissant
Le Lézarde (The Ripening)

contents

one

The Divided Child

An old story goes that Cimabue was struck with
admiration when he saw the shepherd boy, Giotto,
sketching sheep. But, according to the true biographies,
it is never the sheep that inspire a Giotto with the love
of painting: but, rather, his first sight of the paintings of
such a man as Cimabue. What makes the artist is the
circumstance that in his youth he was more deeply
moved by the sight of works of art than by that of the
things which they portray.

Malraux
Psychology of Art

chapter 1

Verandahs, where the pages of the sea
are a book left open by an absent master
in the middle of another life—
I begin here again,
begin until this ocean's
a shut book, and, like a bulb
the white moon's filaments wane.

Begin with twilight, when a glare
which held a cry of bugles lowered
the coconut lances of the inlet,
as a sun, tired of empire, declined.
It mesmerised like fire without wind,
and as its amber climbed
the beer-stein ovals of the British fort
above the promontory, the sky
grew drunk with light.
                                    There
was your heaven! The clear
glaze of another life,
a landscape locked in amber, the rare
gleam. The dream
of reason had produced its monster:
a prodigy of the wrong age and colour.

All afternoon the student
with the dry fever of some draughtsman's clerk
had magnified the harbour, now twilight
eager to complete itself,
drew a girl's figure to the open door
of a stone boathouse with a single stroke, then fell
to a reflecting silence. This silence waited
for the verification of detail:
the gables of the Saint Antoine Hotel
aspiring from jungle, the flag
at Government House melting its pole,
and for the tidal amber glare to glaze
the last shacks of the Morne till they became
transfigured sheerly by the student's will,
a cinquecento fragment in gilt frame.

The vision died,
the black hills simplified
to hunks of coal,
but if the light was dying through the stone
of that converted boathouse on the pier,
a girl, blowing its embers in her kitchen,
could feel its epoch entering her hair.

Darkness, soft as amnesia, furred the slope.
He rose and climbed towards the studio.
The last hill burned,
the sea crinkled like foil,
a moon ballooned up from the Wireless Station. O
mirror, where a generation yearned
for whiteness, for candour, unreturned.

The moon maintained her station,
her fingers stroked a chiton-fluted sea,
her disc whitewashed the shells
of gutted offices barnacling the wharves
of the burnt town, her lamp
baring the ovals of toothless façades,
along the Roman arches, as he passed
her alternating ivories lay untuned,
her age was dead, her sheet
shrouded the antique furniture, the mantel
with its plaster-of-Paris Venus, which
his yearning had made marble, half-cracked
unsilvering mirror of black servants,
like the painter's kerchiefed, ear-ringed portrait: Albertina.

Within the door, a bulb
haloed the tonsure of a reader crouched
in its pale tissue like an embryo,
the leisured gaze
turned towards him, the short arms
yawned briefly, welcome. Let us see.
Brown, balding, a lacertilian
jut to its underlip,
with spectacles thick as a glass paperweight
over eyes the hue of sea-smoothed bottle glass,
the man wafted the drawing to his face
as if dusk were myopic, not his gaze.
Then, with slow strokes the master changed the sketch.

ii

In its dimension the drawing could not trace
the sociological contours of the promontory;
once, it had been an avenue of palms
strict as Hobbema's aisle of lowland poplars,
now, levelled, bulldozed and metalled for an airstrip,
its terraces like tree-rings told its age.
There, patriarchal banyans,
bearded with vines from which black schoolboys gibboned,
brooded on a lagoon seasoned with dead leaves,
mangroves knee-deep in water
crouched like whelk-pickers on brown, spindly legs
scattering red soldier crabs
scrabbling for redcoats' meat.
The groves were sawn
symmetry and contour crumbled,
down the arched barrack balconies
where colonels in the whisky-coloured light
had watched the green flash, like a lizard's tongue,
catch the last sail, tonight
row after row of orange stamps repeated
the villas of promoted Civil Servants.

The moon came to the window and stayed there.
He was her subject, changing when she changed,
from childhood he'd considered palms
ignobler than imagined elms,
the breadfruit's splayed
leaf coarser than the oak's,
he had prayed

6

nightly for his flesh to change,
his dun flesh peeled white by her lightning strokes!
Above the cemetery where
the airstrip's tarmac ended
her slow disc magnified
the life beneath her like a reading-glass.

Below the bulb
a green book, laid
face downward. Moon,
and sea. He read
the spine. FIRST POEMS:
CAMPBELL. The painter
almost absently
reversed it, and began to read:

>   "Holy be
>   the white head of a Negro,
>   sacred be
>   the black flax of a black child . . ."

And from a new book,
bound in sea-green linen, whose lines
matched the exhilaration which their reader,
rowing the air around him now, conveyed,
another life it seemed would start again
while past the droning, tonsured head
the white face
of a dead child stared from its window-frame.

iii

They sang, against the rasp and cough of shovels,
against the fists of mud pounding the coffin,
the diggers' wrists rounding off every phrase,
their iron hymn, "The Pilgrims of the Night."
In the sea-dusk, the live child waited
for the other to escape, a flute
of frail, seraphic mist,
but their black, Bible-paper voices fluttered shut, silence
re-entered every mould, it wrapped the edges
of sea-eaten stone, mantled the blind
eternally gesturing angels, strengthened the flowers
with a different patience, and left
or lost its hoarse voice in the shells
that trumpeted from the graves. The world
stopped swaying and settled in its place.
A black lace glove swallowed his hand.
The engine of the sea began again.

A night-black hearse, tasselled and heavy, lugged
an evening of blue smoke across the field,
like an old wreath the mourners broke apart
and drooped like flowers over the streaked stones
deciphering dates. The gravekeeper with his lantern-jaw
(years later every lantern-swinging porter
guarding infinite rails repeated this), opened
the yellow doorway to his lodge. Wayfarer's station.
The child's journey was signed.
The ledger drank its entry.
Outside the cemetery gates life stretched from sleep.

Gone to her harvest of flax-headed angels,
of seraphs blowing pink-palated conchs,
gone, so they sang, into another light:
But was it her?
Or Thomas Alva Lawrence's dead child,
another Pinkie, in her rose gown floating?
Both held the same dark eyes,
slow, haunting coals, the same curved
ivory hand touching the breast,
as if, answering death, each whispered "Me?"

      iv

Well, everything whitens,
all that town's characters, its cast of thousands
arrested in one still!
As if a sudden flashbulb showed their deaths.
The trees, the road he walks home, a white film,
tonight in the park the children leap into statues,
their outcries round as moonlight,
their flesh like flaking stone,
poor negatives!
They have soaked too long in the basin of the mind,
they have drunk the moon-milk
that X-rays their bodies,
the bone tree shows
through the starved skins,
and one has left, too soon,
a reader out of breath,
and once that begins, how shall I tell them,
while the tired filaments of another moon,
one that was younger,
fades, with the elate extinction of a bulb?

chapter 2

At every first communion, the moon
would lend her lace to a barefooted town
christened, married and buried in borrowed white,
in fretwork borders of carpenter's Gothic,
in mansard bonnets, pleated jalousies,
when, with her laces laid aside,
she was a servant, her sign
a dry park of disconsolate palms, like brooms,
planted by the Seventh Edward, Prince of Wales,
with drooping ostrich crests, ICH DIEN, I SERVE.

I sweep. I iron. The smell of drizzled asphalt
like a flat-iron burning,
odours of smoke, the funereal berried ferns
that made an undertaker's parlour of our gallery.
Across the pebbled back yard, woodsmoke thins,
epiphany of ascension. The soul, like fire,
abhors what it consumes. In the upstairs rooms
smell of blue soap that puckered the black nurse's palms,
those hands which held our faces like a vase;
the coffee-grinder, grumbling,
ground its teeth,
waking at six.
    The cracked egg hisses.

The sheets of Monday
are fluttering from the yard.
The week sets sail.

ii

                Maman,
only on Sundays was the Singer silent,
then,
tobacco smelt stronger, was more masculine.
Sundays
the parlour smelt of uncles,
the lamppoles rang,
the drizzle shivered its maracas,
like mandolins the tightening wires of rain,
then
from striped picnic buses, *jour marron,*
gold bangles tinkled like good-morning in Guinea
and a whore's laughter opened like sliced fruit.

Maman,
you sat folded in silence,
as if your husband might walk up the street,
while in the forests the cicadas pedalled their machines,
and silence, a black maid in white,
barefooted, polished and repolished
the glass across his fading water-colours,
the dumb Victrola cabinet,
the panels and the gleam of blue-winged teal
beating the mirror's lake.
In silence,
the revered, silent objects ring like glass,

11

at my eyes' touch, everything tightened, tuned,
Sunday,
the dead Victrola;

Sunday, a child
breathing with lungs of bread;
Sunday, the sacred silence of machines.

Mama,
your son's ghost circles your lost house, looking in
incomprehensibly at its dumb tenants
like fishes busily inaudible behind glass,
while the carpenter's Gothic joke, A, W, A, W,
Warwick and Alix involved in its eaves
breaks with betrayal.
You stitched us clothes from the nearest elements,
made shirts of rain and freshly ironed clouds,
then, singing your iron hymn, you riveted
your feet on Monday to the old machine.

Then Monday plunged her arms up to the elbows
in a foam tub, under a blue-soap sky,
the wet fleets sailed the yard, and every bubble
with its bent, mullioned window, opened
its mote of envy in the child's green eye
of that sovereign-headed, pink-cheeked bastard Bubbles
in the frontispiece of Pears Cyclopedia.
Rising in crystal spheres, world after world.

They melt from you, your sons.
Your arms grow full of rain.

iii

Old house, old woman, old room,
old planes, old buckling membranes of the womb,
translucent walls,
breathe through your timbers; gasp
arthritic, curling beams,
cough in old air
shining with motes, stair
polished and repolished by the hands of strangers,
die with defiance flecking your grey eyes,
motes of a sunlit air,
your timbers humming with constellations of carcinoma,
your bed frames glowing with radium,
cold iron dilating the fever of your body,
while the galvanised iron snaps in spasms of pain,
but a house gives no outcry,
it bears the depth of forest, of ocean and mother.
Each consuming the other
with memory and unuse.

Why should we weep for dumb things?

This radiance of sharing extends to the simplest objects,
to a favourite hammer, a paintbrush, a toothless,
gum-sunken old shoe,
to the brain of a childhood room, retarded,
lobotomised of its furniture,
stuttering its inventory of accidents:
why this chair cracked,
when did the tightened scream

of that bedspring finally snap,
when did that unsilvering mirror finally
surrender her vanity,
and, in turn, these objects assess us,
that yellow paper flower with the eyes of a cat,
that stain, familiar as warts or some birthmark,
as the badge of some loved defect,

while the thorns of the bougainvillea
moult like old fingernails,
and the flowers keep falling,
and the flowers keep opening,
the allamandas' fallen bugles, but nobody charges.

Skin wrinkles like paint,
the forearm of a balustrade freckles,
crows' feet radiate
from the shut eyes of windows,
and the door, mouth clamped, reveals nothing,
for there is no secret,
there is no other secret
but a pain so alive that
to touch every ledge of that house edges a scream
from the burning wires, the nerves
with their constellation of cancer,
the beams with their star-seed of lice,
pain shrinking every room,
pain shining in every womb,
while the blind, dumb
termites, with jaws of the crabcells consume,
in silent thunder,

to the last of all Sundays,
consume.

Finger each object, lift it
from its place, and it screams again
to be put down
in its ring of dust, like the marriage finger
frantic without its ring;
I can no more move you from your true alignment,
mother, than we can move objects in paintings.

Your house sang softly of balance,
of the rightness of placed things.

chapter 3

Each dusk the leaf flared on its iron tree,
the lamplighter shouldered his ladder, a sickle
of pale light fell on the curb.

The child tented his cotton nightdress tight
across his knees. A kite
whose twigs showed through. Twilight
enshrined the lantern of his head.

Hands swing him heavenward.
The candle's yellow leaf next to his bed
re-letters *Tanglewood Tales* and Kingsley's *Heroes*,
gilding their backs,

the ceiling reels with magic lantern shows.
The black lamplighter with Demeter's torch
ignites the iron trees above the shacks.
Boy! Who was Ajax?

ii

Ajax,
   lion-coloured stallion from Sealey's stable,
   by day a cart-horse, a thoroughbred

on race-days, once a year,
plunges the thunder of his neck, and sniffs
above the garbage smells, the scent
of battle, and the shouting,
he saith among the kitchen peels "Aha!"
debased, bored animal,
its dung cakes pluming, gathers
the thunder of its flanks, and drags
its chariot to the next block, where

Berthilia,
    the frog-like, crippled crone,
    a hump on her son's back, is carried
    to her straw mat, her day-long perch,
    Cassandra, with her drone unheeded.
    Her son, Pierre, carries night-soil in buckets,
    she spurs him like a rider,
    horsey-back, horsey-back;
    when he describes his cross he sounds content,
    he is everywhere admired. A model son.

Choiseul,
    surly chauffeur from Clauzel's garage,
    bangs Troy's gate shut!
    It hinges on a scream. His rusty
    commonlaw wife's. Hands hard as a crank handle,
    he is obsequious, in love with engines.
    They can be reconstructed. Before
    human complications, his horny hands are thumbs.
    Now, seal your eyes, and think of Homer's grief.

Darnley,
>skin freckled like a mango leaf,
>feels the sun's fingers press his lids.
>His half-brother Russell steers him by the hand.
>Seeing him, I practise blindness.
>Homer and Milton in their owl-blind towers,
>I envy him his great affliction. Sunlight
>whitens him like a negative.

Emanuel
>Auguste, out in the harbour, lone Odysseus,
>tattooed ex-merchant sailor, rows alone
>through the rosebloom of dawn to chuckling oars
>measured, dip, pentametrical, reciting
>through narrowed eyes as his blades scissor silk,

>>"Ah moon / (bend, stroke)
>>of my delight / (bend, stroke)
>>that knows no wane.
>>The moon of heaven / (bend, stroke)
>>is rising once again,"

>defiling past Troy town, his rented oars
>remembering what seas, what smoking shores?

FARAH & RAWLINS, temple with
>plate-glass front, gutted, but girded by
>Ionic columns, before which mincing

Gaga
>the town's transvestite, housemaid's darling,

is window-shopping, swirling his plastic bag,
before his houseboy's roundtrip to Barbados,
most Greek of all, the love that hath no name, and

Helen?
    Janie, the town's one clear-complexioned whore,
    with two tow-headed children in her tow,
    she sleeps with sailors only, her black
    hair electrical
    as all that trouble over Troy,
    rolling broad-beamed she leaves
    a plump and pumping vacancy,
    "O promise me," as in her satin sea-heave follow
    cries of

Ityn! Tin! Tin!
    from Philomène, the bird-brained idiot girl,
    eyes skittering as the sea-swallow
    since her rape,
    laying on lust, in her unspeakable tongue,
    her silent curse.

Joumard,
    the fowl-thief with his cockerel's strut,
    heads home like Jason, in his fluttering coat
    a smoke-drugged guinea-hen,
    the golden fleece,

Kyrie! kyrie! twitter
    a choir of surpliced blackbirds in the pews
    of telephone wires, bringing day to

Ligier,
    reprieved murderer, tangled in his pipe smoke
    wrestling Laocoön,
    bringing more gold to

Midas,
    Monsieur Auguste Manoir,
    pillar of business and the Church
    rising to watch the sunlight work for him,
    gilding the wharf's warehouses with his name.

Nessus,
    nicknamed N'homme Maman Migrain
    (your louse's mother's man),
    rises in sackcloth, prophesying
    fire and brimstone on the gilt wooden towers of
    offices, ordures, on
    Peter & Co. to burn like Pompeii, on J.
    Q. Charles's stores, on the teetering, scabrous City of
    Refuge, my old grandmother's barracks, where, once

Submarine,
    the seven-foot-high bum-boatman,
    loose, lank and gangling as a frayed cheroot,
    once asking to see a ship's captain, and refused,
    with infinite courtesy bending, inquired
    "So what the hell is your captain?
    A fucking microbe?"

Troy town awakens,
    in its shirt of fire, but on our street

Uncle Eric
    sits in a shadowed corner,
    mumbling, hum-eyed,
    writing his letters to the world,
    his tilted hand scrambling for foothold.

Vaughan,
    battling his itch, waits for the rumshop's
    New Jerusalem, while Mister

Weekes,
    slippered black grocer in gold-rimmed spectacles,
    paddles across a rug of yellow sunshine
    laid at his feet by the shadows of tall houses,
    towards his dark shop,
    propelled in his tranced passage by one star:
    Garvey's imperial emblem of Africa United,
    felt slippers muttering in Barbadian brogue,
    and, entering his shop,
    is mantled like a cleric
    in a soutane of onion smells, saltfish and garlic,
    salt-flaked Newfoundland cod hacked by a cleaver
    on a scarred counter where a bent half-penny
    shows Edward VII, Defender of the Faith, Emperor of India,
    next to a Lincoln penny, IN GOD WE TRUST
    "and in God one, b' Christ," thinks Mr. Weekes,
    opening his Bible near the paradise plums,
    arm crooked all day over a window open
    at the New Jerusalem, for Coloured People Only.
    At Exodus.

Xodus, bearing back the saxophonist,
     Yes, whose ramshorn is his dented saxophone,
     bearing back to the green grasses of Guinea,

Zandoli,
     nicknamed The Lizard,
     rodent-exterminator, mosquito-murderer,
     equipment slung over a phthisic shoulder,
     safariing from Mary Ann Street's café,
     wiping a gum-bright grin, out for the week's assault on
     roaches, midges, jiggers, rodents, bugs and larvae,
     singing, refumigating
     Jerusalem, for Coloured People Only.

     These dead, these derelicts,
     that alphabet of the emaciated,
     they were the stars of my mythology.

chapter 4

—Jerusalem, the golden,
With milk and honey blest

Thin water glazed
        the pebbled knuckles of the Baptist's feet.
In Craven's book.
Their haloes shone like the tin guards of lamps.
Verocchio. Leonardo painted the kneeling angel's hair.
Kneeling in our plain chapel,
I envied them their frescoes.
Italy flung round my shoulders like a robe,
I ran among dry rocks, howling, "Repent!"
Zinnias, or else some coarser marigold,
brazenly rigid in their metal bowls
or our porch's allamandas trumpeted
from the Vermeer white napery of the altar:
LET US COME INTO HIS PRESENCE WITH THANKSGIVING
AND INTO HIS COURTS WITH PRAISE.
        Those bowls,
in whose bossed brass the stewards were repeated
and multiplied, as in an insect's eye,
some jewelled insect in a corner of Crivelli,
were often ours, as were the trumpet flowers
between the silvered chargers with the Host
and ruby blood.

Collect, epistle, lesson,
the Jacobean English rang, new-minted,
the speech of simple men,
evangelists, reformers, abolitionists,
their text was cold brook water,
they fell to foreign fevers,
I would be a preacher,
I would write great hymns.

Arnold, staid melancholy of those Sabbath dusks,
I know those rigorous teachers of your youth,
Victorian gravures of the Holy Land,
thorn-tortured Palestine,
bearded disciples wrapped tight in malaria,
the light of desert fevers,
and those thin sunsets
with the consistency of pumpkin soup.
Grey chapel where parched and fiery Reverend Pilgrims
were shrieking twigs,
frock-coated beetles gesturing hell-fire.
Are you cast down, cast down, my coal-black kin?
Be not afraid, the Lord shall raise you up.

The cloven hoof, the hairy paw
despite the passionate, pragmatic
Methodism of my infancy,
crawled through the thicket of my hair,
till sometimes the skin prickled
even in sunshine at "negromancy";
traumatic, tribal,
an atavism stronger than their Mass,
stronger than chapel, whose

tubers gripped the rooted middle-class,
beginning where Africa began:
in the body's memory.

I knew them all,
the "swell-foot," the epileptic *"mal-cadi,"*
cured by stinking compounds,
tisane, bush-bath, the exhausting emetic,
and when these failed, the incurably sored and sick
brought in a litter to the obeah-man.
One step beyond the city was the bush.
One step behind the churchdoor stood the devil.

THE PACT

One daybreak, as the iron light,
which guards dawn like a shopfront, lifted,
a scavenger washing the gutters stood
dumbstruck at the cross
where Chaussee Road and Grass Street intersect
before a rusting bloodstain.
A bubbling font at which
a synod of parsonical flies presided,
washing their hands. The scavenger Zandoli
slowly crossed himself.
The slowly sinking stain mapped no direction
in which the thing, a dog, perhaps, had crawled.
Light flushed its crimson like an obscene rose.
A knot of black communicants,
mainly old women, chorused round the wound.
The asphalt, like an artery, flowed, unstanched.

Monsieur Auguste Manoir, pillar of the Church,
lay on his back and watched dawn ring
his bed's gold quoits, and gild the view
of hills and roofs the hue of crusted blood,
heard the grey, iron harbour
open on a sea-gull's rusty hinge,
and knew, as soundlessly as sunlight,
that today he would die.

The blood of garbage mongrels had a thin,
watery excretion; this, a rich red
bubbled before their eyes.

Monsieur Manoir
urged his ringed, hairy hand to climb his stomach
to nuzzle at his heart.
Its crabbed jaw clenched the crucifix;
he heaved there, wheezing,
in the pose of one swearing eternal fealty,
hearing his blood race
like wine from a barrel when its bung has burst.

The blood coagulated like dregged wine.
Zandoli hefted a bucket
washing it wide. It
spread like a dying crab, clenching the earth.
Laved in a sudden wash of sweat, Manoir
struggled to scream for help.
His wife, in black, bent at communion.
Released, he watched the light deliriously dancing
on the cold, iron roofs of his warehouses
whose corrugations rippled with his name.

His hands still smelled of fish, of his beginnings,
hands that he'd ringed with gold, to hide their smell,
sometimes he'd hold them out,
puckered with lotions, powdered, to his wife,
a peasant's hands, a butcher's,
their acrid odour of saltfish and lard.
Drawn by the sweat,
a fly prayed at his ear-well:

Bon Dieu, pardon,
Demou, merci,
l'odeur savon,
l'odeur parfum
pas sait guérir
l'odeur péché,
l'odeur d'enfer,
pardonnez-moi
Auguste Manoir!

If there was one thing Manoir's watchman hated
more than the merchant, it was the merchant's dog,
more wolf than dog. It would break loose
some nights, rooting at the warehouse,
paws scuffing dirt like hands for some lost bone.
Before he struck it, something dimmed its eyes.
Its head dilating like an obscene rose,
humming and gemmed with flies, the dog
tottered through the tiled hallway of the house
towards its bed.

Under a scabrous roof whose fences
held the colours of dried blood, Saylie,

27

the wrinkled washerwoman, howled
in gibberish, in the devil's Latin.
Stepping back from the stench
as powerful as a cloud of smoke
the young priest chanted:
per factotem mundi,
per eum qui habet potestatem
mittendi te in gehennam . . .
six men with difficulty pinning her down,
gasping like divers coming up for breath,
her wild eyes rocketing,
as Beherit and Eazaz wrestled in her smoke.

The stores opened for business.
A stench of rumour filtered through the streets.
He was the first black merchant baron.
They would say things, of course, they would think things,
those children of his fellow villagers
descending the serpentine roads from the Morne,
they'd say his name in whispers now, "Manoir."

The priest prayed swiftly, averting his head,
she had, he knew, contracted with the devil,
now, dying, his dog's teeth tugged at her soul
like cloth in a wringer when the cogs have caught,
their hands pulled at its stuff through her clenched teeth,
"Name him!" The priest intoned, "Name! *Déparlez!*"
The bloodstain in the street dried quick as sweat.
"Manoir," she screamed, "that dog, Auguste Manoir."

chapter 5

—Statio haud malefida carinis

AUGUSTE MANOIR, MERCHANT: LICENSED TO SELL
INTOXICATING LIQUOR, RETAILER, DRY GOODS, etc.
his signs peppered the wharves.
From the canted barracks of the City of Refuge,
from his grandmother's tea-shop, he would watch
on black hills of imported anthracite
the frieze of coal-black carriers, *charbonniers,*
erect, repetitive as hieroglyphs
descending and ascending the steep ramps,
building the pyramids,
songs of Egyptian bondage,
                        when they sang,
the burden of the panniered anthracite,
one hundredweight to every woman
tautened, like cable, the hawsers in their necks.
There was disease inhaled in the coal-dust.
Silicosis. Herring-gulls
white as the uniforms of tally clerks,
screeching, numbered and tagged the loads.

"Boy! Name the great harbours of the world!"
"Sydney! Sir."

29

"San Fransceesco!"
"Naples, sah!"
"And what about Castries?"
"Sah, Castries ees a coaling station and
der twenty-seventh best harba in der worl'!
In eet the entire Breetesh Navy can be heeden!"
"What is the motto of Saint Lucia, boy?"
"*Statio haud malefida carinis.*"
"Sir!"
"Sir!"
"And what does that mean?"
"Sir, a safe anchorage for sheeps!"

High on the Morne,
flowers medalled the gravestones of the Inniskillings,
too late. Bamboos burst like funereal gunfire.
Noon smoke of cannon fodder,
as black bat cries recited Vergil's tag: "*Statio haud!*"
Safe in their anchorage, sloe-lidded sloops
admired their reflections: *Phyllis Mark,*
Albertha Compton, Lady Joy, The Jewel.

ii

The teetering two-storeyed house next door became a haven
for bat-like transients.
Tenants flashed in and out of its dark rooms.
Their cries shot from its eaves. A family of creoles.
The mother a yellow, formidable Martiniquaise,
handsome, obliquely masculine, with a mole, "*très égyptienne,*"
black sapodilla-seed eyes

under the ziggurat of her pompadour,
we called "The Captain's Wife."

Sometimes, when the wind's hand creaked her upstairs window open,
hiding in the dim angle of our bedroom
I'd try to catch her naked. Their son, Gentile,
had round, scared eyes, a mouth
that gibbered in perpetual terror,
even in sunshine he shivered like a foundling.
"Gentile, Gentile!" we called. His own name frightened him.

We all knew when the Captain had dry-docked.
There would be violent bursts of shrieking French,
and in my own bed, parallel, separated by a gulf
of air, I'd hear the Captain's Wife,
sobbing, denying.
Next day her golden face seemed shrunken,
then, when he ulysseed, she bloomed again,
the bat-swift transients returned,
so many, perhaps they quartered in the eaves.
Dressed in black lace, like an impatient widow,
I imagined that skin, pomegranate, under silks
the sheen of water, and that
sweet-sour stink vixens give off.

Serene, and unimaginably naked,
as her dark countrymen hung round her rooms,
we heard their laughter tinkling above the glasses.
They came when Foquarde travelled down the coast.
Her laugh rang like the jangling of bracelets.

iii

Jewel, a single stack, diesel, forty-foot coastal vessel,
its cabin curtained with canvas meant to shield
passengers from the sun,
but through which rain and shining spray still drenched,
coughed like a relic out of Conrad. Twice a week
she loaded her cargo of pigs, charcoal, food, lumber,
squabbling or frightened peasants, the odd priest,
threading the island's jettied villages,
Anse-la-Raye, Canaries, Soufrière, Choiseul,
and back. She also carried mail.

In deepgreen village coves she rocked offshore,
threatening her breakdown,
while rust bled from her wash,
a litter of dugouts nuzzling at her flank,
off-loading goods and passengers.

Disembarkation was precarious,
the inshore swell had to be nicely timed,
against the lunge of struggling canoes
in which, feet planted squarely as a mast, one man
stood, swaying, heaving with the swell.

iv

Her course sheared perilously close to the ochre rocks
and bushy outcrops of the leeward coast,
sometimes so closely that it seemed to us
"that all the shoreline's leaves were magnified

deliberately, with frightening detail,"
yet the yellow coast uncoiling past her prow
like new rope from a bollard never lost interest,
especially when the coiled beach lay
between black coves blinding
half-moon of sand,
before some settlement which the passengers
however often they had made this journey
always gave different names,
"because it went on repeating itself exactly,"
palms, naked children fishing, wretched huts,
a stone church by a brown, clogged river,
the leper colony of Malgrétoute.

A church, hedged by an unconverted forest,
a beach without a footprint, clear or malformed,
no children, no one, on the hollow pier.
The Jewel hove to, ringing her leper's bell.
The passengers crossed themselves and turned,
inevitably, to the priest.
He'd rise as the canoe appeared.
Condemned. I searched his skin.
The surpliced water heaved.
The bell tinkled like Mass. The priest got off.

He sat still in the long canoe, the afternoon
swallowed the bell-rings slowly,
one hand steadying his hat,
the other gripping its stern.
After a while we lost him to the dark green
ocean of the leaves, a white speck, a sail,
out of our memory and our gratitude.

chapter 6

Surpliced, processional,
the shallows mutter in Latin,
maris stella, maris stella,

lichens of leprosy,
disconsolate plumes
of the cabbage palms' casques,

alleluia!

Oversexed cockerel,
cutthroat of dawn,
rattle your wattle,

gloria!

A mast tied with flowers
marries canoe and river,
ora!

The bell-mouth of twilight
chafes like a sore,

serene eye of blue
blind, flaking on rock-prow,

foam-snooded figurehead
with her foam-plume lily,
maris stella.

Maria, Maria,
your bows nod benediction,
the broken pier kneels,

sanctus, sanctus,
from the tonsured mountains
the slow stink of incense

from Soufrière's chancre
the volcano's
sulphurous censer,

Sancta Lucia,
an island brittle
as a Lenten biscuit,

a map of cracked precipices
un pain d'épice
christened by Vergil,

*statio haud
malefida carinis,*
screaking from pulleys

35

the sail's abrupt sanctus.
Vespers. From chapel
the tinkle of a sheep's bell

draws the sea-flocks homeward.

ii

At Canaries,
the sea's steel razor
shines.

Broken, decrepit port
for some rum-eyed romantic,
his empire's secret rusting in a sea-chest,

tarred, tattered coconuts,
an exile's niche
for some Tuan Jim, "a water-clerk under a cloud"

(The T.L.S.).
Roofs of tin,
pray for us.
The one bell bangs. Too loud.

At Anse-la-Raye,
moving among pot-stomached, dribbling, snotted,
starved, fig-navelled, mud-baked cherubim,
the French priest strolls down to the pier.
The Jewel,

rounding the point, bringing mail,

the unfinished Government road
"right round the island," will not be finished this year.

A fish plops. Making rings
that marry the wide harbour.
Navel of life. Perhaps he should have married.

His head is a burnt shell.
This was his heaven once. It smells like hell.
"And what is hell, my children?"

Qui côté c'est l'enfer?
Why, Father, on this coast.
Father, hell is

two hundred shacks on wooden stilts,
one bushy path to the night-soil pits.

Hell is this hole where the devil shits,
but tinkle your mission bell,
M.V. *Jewel*, for

Soufrière, where
the raw
sore of the volcano chafes,
exhausted boil.
Maleboge, where some golden Louis
buried his soldiers,
where the green fusiliers boiled themselves like lobsters,
their ranks bled white,
mute clangour now under the metal leaves
the golden cocoa's tattered epaulettes,

Alouette, gentille alouette,
tune of the Lark's legions gone to hack pasta,
Louis, their sun-king, sinking
like metal coins under the black leaves,
the stink of sulphur unendurable,
like Marat's bath-pit.
That very special reek,
tristes, tristes tropiques.

Under the Pitons, the green
bay, dark as oil.
Breasts of a woman, serenely rising.
Thought Capitaine Foquarde,
"This is good soil."

iii

Palm trunks irregular as railings fenced the beaches.
Behind them: private property, the island quartered
into baronial estates, gone, gone,
their golden, bugled epoch.
Aubrey Smith characters in khaki helmets,
Victorian flourish of oratorical moustaches.
Retired Captain X, who kept an open grave behind his house,
would shoot on sight. Shot himself, sah!
B. reputedly galloped his charger through the canes,
pointed his whip at nubile coolie girls, "Up to the house,"
droit de seigneur, keeping employment in the family.
Timid, bespectacled Monsieur D., more bank-clerk than sugar-baron,
piety on a horse,
and Royer was murdered in dark cocoa-bushes, Boscobel,
by three niggers stealing his coconuts.

The air there, stained. Furred. Soft as tarantulas
scuttling the hairy cocoa-leaves.
Baron, ship-chandler, merchant, water-clerk,
the fiction of their own lives claimed each one.
My fiery grandfather,
his house burnt at Choiseul, and he inside it.
Froth of malaria on the pool's lip.
Bilharzia enters the intestines of small children,
a sort of river tsetse, mines, in the guts,
in labourers, producing lethargy. "We cure it,"
said the young research scientist,
"and multiply the unemployment problem."

iv

Heureux qui comme Ulysse,
ou Capitaine Foquarde,
while his pomegranate skinned
Martiniquan Penelope
rocks in her bentwood chair,
laughing, stitching ripped knickers,
as her coast-threading captain
hums, *"La vie c'est un voyage"*
and the polished rocker dips
as her white burst of laughter
drives deep whose prow?

Pigs bring bad luck. And priests.
The shorn priest sat to starboard,
cowled by torn canvas,
numbering the beads of villages,
Foquarde. Coquarde.

Lost, lost, rain-hidden, precipitous, debased,
ocean's soiled lace around her dirty ankles.
The ship's bell rankled. At the greased wheel
Foquarde turned, looking seaward.

A tanker.
       Her red, dipping prow,
                        a mouth,
remembering the names of islands.

chapter 7

Provincialism loves the pseudo-epic,
so if these heroes have been given a stature
disproportionate to their cramped lives,
remember I beheld them at knee-height,
and that their thunderous exchanges
rumbled like gods about another life,
as now, I hope, some child
ascribes their grandeur to Gregorias.
Remember years must pass before he saw an orchestra,
a train, a theatre, the spark-coloured leaves
of autumn whirling from a rail-line,
that, as for the seasons,
the works he read described their passage with
processional arrogance; then pardon, life,
if he saw autumn in a rusted leaf.
What else was he but a divided child?

I saw, as through the glass of some provincial gallery
the hieratic objects which my father loved:
the stuffed dark nightingale of Keats,
bead-eyed, snow-headed eagles,
all that romantic taxidermy,
and each one was a fragment of the True Cross,
each one upheld, as if it were The Host;

those venerated, venerable objects
borne by the black hands (reflecting like mahogany)
of reverential teachers, shone the more
they were repolished by our use.

The Church upheld the Word, but this new Word
was here, attainable
to my own hand,
in the deep country it found the natural man,
generous, rooted.
And I now yearned to suffer for that life,
I looked for some ancestral, tribal country,
I heard its clear tongue over the clean stones
of the river, I looked from the bus-window
and multiplied the bush with savages,
speckled the leaves with jaguar and deer,
I changed those crusted boulders
to grey, stone-lidded crocodiles,
my head shrieked with metallic, raucous parrots,
I held my breath as savages grinned,
stalking, through the bush.

ii

About the August of my fourteenth year
I lost my self somewhere above a valley
owned by a spinster-farmer, my dead father's friend.
At the hill's edge there was a scarp
with bushes and boulders stuck in its side.
Afternoon light ripened the valley,
rifling smoke climbed from small labourers' houses,
and I dissolved into a trance.

I was seized by a pity more profound
than my young body could bear, I climbed
with the labouring smoke,
I drowned in labouring breakers of bright cloud,
then uncontrollably I began to weep,
inwardly, without tears, with a serene extinction
of all sense; I felt compelled to kneel,
I wept for nothing and for everything,
I wept for the earth of the hill under my knees,
for the grass, the pebbles, for the cooking smoke
above the labourers' houses like a cry,
for unheard avalanches of white cloud,
but "darker grows the valley, more and more forgetting."
For their lights still shine through the hovels like litmus,
the smoking lamp still slowly says its prayer,
the poor still move behind their tinted scrim,
the taste of water is still shared everywhere,
but in that ship of night, locked in together,
through which, like chains, a little light might leak,
something still fastens us forever to the poor.

But which was the true light?
Blare noon or twilight,
"the lonely light that Samuel Palmer engraved,"
or the cold
iron entering the soul, as the soul sank
out of belief.
                    That bugle-coloured twilight
blew the withdrawal not of legions and proconsuls,
but of pale, prebendary clerks, with the gait and gall
of camels. And yet I envied them,
bent, silent decipherers of sacred texts,

their Roman arches, Vergilian terraces,
their tiered, ordered colonial world
where evening, like the talons of a bird
bent the blue jacaranda softly, and smoke rose with
the leisure and frailty of recollection,
I learnt their strict necrology of dead kings,
bones freckling the rushes of damp tombs,
the light-furred luminous world of Claude,
their ruined temples, and in drizzling twilights, Turner.

     iii

Our father,
       who floated in the vaults of Michelangelo,
Saint Raphael,
       of sienna and gold leaf,
it was then
       that he fell in love, having no care
for truth,
       that he could enter the doorway of a triptych,
that he believed
       those three stiff horsemen cantering past a rock,
       towards jewelled cities on a cracked horizon,
       that the lances of Uccello shivered him,
       like Saul, unhorsed,
that he fell in love with art,
       and life began.

     iv

Noon,
       and its sacred water sprinkles.

44

A schoolgirl in blue and white uniform,
her golden plaits a simple coronet
out of Angelico, a fine sweat on her forehead,
hair where the twilight singed and signed its epoch.
And a young man going home.
They move away from each other.
They are moving towards each other.
His head roars with hunger and poems.
His hand is trembling to recite her name.
She clutches her books, she is laughing,
her uniformed companions laughing.
She laughs till she is near tears.

                v

Who could tell, in "the crossing of that pair"
            that later it would mean
that rigid iron lines were drawn between
            him and that garden chair
from which she rose to greet him, as for a train,
            that watching her rise
from the bright boathouse door was like some station
            where either stood, transfixed
by the rattling telegraph of carriage windows
            flashing goodbyes,
that every dusk rehearsed a separation
            already in their eyes,
that later, when they sat in silence, seaward,
            and looking upward, heard
its engines as some moonlit liner chirred
            from the black harbour outward,
those lights spelt out their sentence, word by word?

two

Homage to Gregorias

I saw them growing gaunt and pale in their unlighted
studios. The Indian turning green, the Negro's smile
gone, the white man more perverted—more and more
forgetful of the sun they had left behind, trying des-
perately to imitate what came naturally to those whose
rightful place was in the net. Years later, having
frittered away their youth, they would return with
vacant eyes, all initiative gone, without heart to set
themselves the only task appropriate to the milieu
that was slowly revealing to me the nature of its
values: Adam's task of giving things their names.

Alejo Carpentier
The Lost Steps

chapter 8

—*West Indian Gothic*

A gaunt, gabled house,
grey, fretted, soars
above a verdigris canal which
sours with moss. A bridge,
lithe as a schoolboy's leap,
vaults the canal. Each
longitudinal window seems *large stone coffin*
a vertical sarcophagus, a niche *resting place with*
in which its family must sleep
erect, repetitive as saints
in their cathedral crypt, *underground chamber*
like urgent angels in their fluted stone
sailing their stone dream.
And like their house,
all the Gregoriases
were pious, arrogant men,
of that first afternoon, when
Gregorias ushered me in there,
I recall an air of bugled orders,
cavalry charges of children
tumbling down the stair,
a bristling, courteous father,

49

but also something delicate,
a dessicating frailty which showed
in his worn mother, a taut tree
shorn to the dark house's use,
its hothouse, fragile atmosphere
labouring yearly to produce
the specimen, *Gregorias elongatus*.

In the spear-lowering light of afternoon
I paced his hunter's stride,
there was a hierarchic arrogance in his bearing
which crested in the martial,
oracular moustaches of his father,
a Lewis gunner in the First World War,
now brown, prehensile fingers plucked his work,
lurid Madonnas, pietistic crucifixions
modelled on common Catholic lithographs,
but with the personal flourish of a witness.
Widowed, his father's interest in life declined,
his battle finished. The brown twigs broke apart.

Around that golden year which I described
Gregorias and that finished soldier quartered
in a brown, broken-down bungalow
whose yard was indistinguishable from bush,
between the broad-leaved jungle and the town.
Shaky, half-rotted treaders, sighing, climbed
towards a sun-warped verandah, one half of which
Gregorias had screened into a studio,
shading a varnished, three-legged table
crawling with exhausted paint-tubes, a lowering quart
of *Pirate* rum, and grey, dog-eared, turpentine-stained editions

of the Old Masters. One day the floor collapsed.
The old soldier sank suddenly to his waist
wearing the verandah like a belt.
Gregorias buckled with laughter telling this,
but shame broke the old warrior.
The dusk lowered his lances through the leaves.
In another year the soldier shrank and died.
Embittered, Gregorias wanted carved on his stone:
PRAISE YOUR GOD, DRINK YOUR RUM, MIND YOUR OWN BUSINESS.

We were both fatherless now, and often drunk.

Drunk,
       on a half-pint of joiner's turpentine,
drunk,
          while the black, black-sweatered, horn-soled fishermen drank
          their *l'absinthe* in sand back yards standing up,
          on the clear beer of sunrise,
          on cheap, tannic Canaries muscatel,
          on glue, on linseed oil, on kerosene,
          as Van Gogh's shadow rippling on a cornfield,
          on Cézanne's boots grinding the stones of Aix
          to shales of slate, ochre and Vigie blue,
          on Gauguin's hand shaking the gin-coloured dew
          from the umbrella yams,
          garrulous, all day, sun-struck,
till dusk glazed vision with its darkening varnish.
Days welded by the sun's torch into days!
Gregorias plunging whole-suit in the shallows,
painting under water, roaring, and spewing spray,
Gregorias gesturing, under the coconuts
wickerwork shade–tin glare–wickerwork shade,

days woven into days, a stinging haze
of thorn trees bent like green flames by the Trades,
under a sky tacked to the horizon, drumskin tight,
as shaggy combers leisurely beard the rocks,
while the asphalt sweats its mirages and the beaks
of fledgling ginger lilies
gasped for rain.
Gregorias, the easel rifled on his shoulder, marching
towards an Atlantic flashing tinfoil,
singing "O Paradiso,"
till the western breakers laboured to that music,
his canvas crucified against a tree.

ii

But drunkenly, or secretly, we swore,
disciples of that astigmatic saint,
that we would never leave the island
until we had put down, in paint, in words,
as palmists learn the network of a hand,
all of its sunken, leaf-choked ravines,
every neglected, self-pitying inlet
muttering in brackish dialect, the ropes of mangroves
from which old soldier crabs slipped
surrendering to slush,
each ochre track seeking some hilltop and
losing itself in an unfinished phrase,
under sand shipyards where the burnt-out palms
inverted the design of unrigged schooners,
entering forests, boiling with life,
goyave, corrosol, bois-canot, sapotille.

Days!
The sun drumming, drumming,
past the defeated pennons of the palms,
roads limp from sunstroke,
past green flutes of grass
the ocean cannonading, come!
Wonder that opened like the fan
of the dividing fronds
on some noon-struck Sahara,
where my heart from its rib-cage yelped like a pup
after clouds of sanderlings rustily wheeling
the world on its ancient,
invisible axis,
the breakers slow-dolphining over more breakers,
to swivel our easels down, as firm
as conquerors who had discovered home.

iii

For no one had yet written of this landscape
that it was possible, though there were sounds
given to its varieties of wood;

the *bois-canot* responded to its echo,
when the axe spoke, weeds ran up to the knee
like bastard children, hiding in their names,

whole generations died, unchristened,
growths hidden in green darkness, forests
of history thickening with amnesia,

53

so that a man's branched, naked trunk,
its roots crusted with dirt,
swayed where it stopped, remembering another name;

breaking a lime leaf,
cracking an acrid ginger-root,
a smell of tribal medicine stained the mind,

stronger than ocean's rags,
than the reek of the maingot forbidden pregnant women,
than the smell of the horizon's rusting rim,

here was a life older than geography,
as the leaves of edible roots opened their pages
at the child's last lesson, Africa, heart-shaped,

and the lost Arawak hieroglyphs and signs
were razed from slates by sponges of the rain,
their symbols mixed with lichen,

the archipelago like a broken root,
divided among tribes, while trees and men
laboured assiduously, silently to become

whatever their given sounds resembled,
ironwood, logwood-heart, golden apples, cedars,
and were nearly

ironwood, logwood-heart, golden apples, cedars,
men . . .

chapter 9

There are already, invisible on canvas,
lines locking into outlines. The visible dissolves
in a benign acid. The leaf
insists on its oval echo, that wall
breaks into sweat, oil settles
in the twin pans of the eyes.

Blue, on the tip of the tongue,
and this cloud can go no further.
Over your shoulder the landscape
frowns at its image. A rigour
of zinc white seizes the wall,
April ignites the immortelle,
the leaf of a kneeling sapling
is the yellow flame of Lippi's Annunciation.
Like the scrape of a struck match, cadmium orange,
evened to the wick of a lantern.
Like a crowd, surrounding the frame
the muttering variegations of green.

The mountain's crouching back begins to ache.

The eyes sweat, small fires gnaw
at the edge of the canvas,

ochre, sienna, their smoke
billows into blue cloud.
A bird's cry tries to pierce
the thick silence of canvas.
From the reeds of your lashes, the wild commas
of crows are beginning to rise.
At your feet
the dead cricket grows into a dragon,
the razor grass bristles resentment,
gnats are sawing the air,
the sun plates your back,
salt singes your eyes
and a crab, the brush in its pincer,
scrapes the white sand of canvas,

as the sea's huge eye stuns you
with the lumbering, oblique blow
of its weary, pelagic eyelid,
its jaw ruminates
on the seagrass it munches
while the lighthouse needle signals
like a stuttering compass
north north by north west north
and your hair roars like an oven
and a cloud passes,
till the landscape settles on
a horizon humming with balance,
and like a tired sitter
the world shifts its weight.

Remember Vincent, saint
of all sunstroke, remember

Paul, their heads
plated with fire!
The sun explodes into irises,
the shadows are crossing like crows,
they settle, clawing the hair,
yellow is screaming.

Dear Theo, I shall go mad.

Is that where it lies,
in the light of that leaf, the glint
of some gully, in a day
glinting with mica, in that rock
that shatters in slate,
in that flashing buckle of ocean?
The skull is sucked dry as a seed,
the landscape is finished.
The ants blacken it, signing.
Round the roar of an oven, the gnats
hiss their finical contradiction.
Nature is a fire,
through the door of this landscape
I have entered a furnace.

I rise, ringing with sunstroke!

The foreground lurches up drunkenly,
the cold sea is coiled in your gut,
the sky's ring dilates, dilates, and
the tongue tastes sand,
the mouth is sour with failure,
the hair on your nape,

spiders running over your wrist,
stirs like trees on the edge of that ridge,
you have eaten nothing but this landscape
all day, from daybreak to noon and past noon
the acrid greens and ochres
rust in the gut.
The stomach heaves, look away.
Your lashes settle like crows.

I have toiled all of life for this failure.
Beyond this frame, deceptive, indifferent,
nature returns to its work,
behind the square of blue you have cut from that sky,
another life, real, indifferent, resumes.
Let the hole heal itself.
The window is shut.
The eyelids cool in the shade.
Nothing will show after this, nothing
except the frame which you carry in your sealed, surrendering eyes.

ii

Where did I fail? I could draw,
I was disciplined, humble, I rendered
the visible world that I saw
exactly, yet it hindered me, for
in every surface I sought
the paradoxical flash of an instant
in which every facet was caught
in a crystal of ambiguities,
I hoped that both disciplines might
by painful accretion cohere

and finally ignite,
but I lived in a different gift,
its element metaphor,
while Gregorias would draw
with the linear elation of an eel
one muscle in one thought,
my hand was crabbed by that style,
this epoch, that school
or the next, it shared
the translucent soul of the fish, while
Gregorias abandoned apprenticeship
to the errors of his own soul,
it was classic versus romantic
perhaps, it was water and fire,
and how often my hand betrayed
creeping across the white sand,
poor crab, its circuitous instinct
to fasten on what it seized,
but I was his runner, I paced him,
I admired the explosion of impulse,
I envied and understood
his mountainous derision
at this sidewise crawling, this classic
condition of servitude.
His work was grotesque, but whole,
and however bad it became
it was his, he possessed
aboriginal force and it came
as the carver comes out of the wood.
Now, every landscape we entered
was already signed with his name.

iii

In my father's small blue library
of reproductions I would find
that fine drawn hare of Durer's, clenched and quivering
to leap across my wrist,
and volumes of *The English Topographical Draughtsmen,*
Peter de Wint, Paul Sandby, Cotman, and in another
sky-blue book
the shepherdesses of Boucher and Fragonard,
and I raved for
the split pears of their arses,
their milk-jug bubs,
the close and, I guessed, golden
inlay of curls at cunt
and conch-like ear,
and after service, Sunday lay
golden, a fucked Eve
replete and apple-bearing,
and if they were my Muse,
still, out of that you rose,
body downed with the seasons,
gold and white, Anna
of the peach-furred body, light
of another epoch,
and stone-grey eyes.
Was the love wrong that came
out of the Book of Hours,
and the reaper with his scythe,
as your hair gold, dress green,
sickle-armed, you move

through a frontispiece of flowers
eternal, true as Ruth
the wheat-sheaves at her ear,
or gorgonizing Judith
swinging the dead lantern
of Holofernes, that bright year
like all first love, we were
pure and Pre-Raphaelite,
Circe-coil of plaited light
around her, as Gregorias
bent to his handful of earth,
his black nudes gleaming sweat,
in the tiger shade of the fronds.

Through the swift year
the canvases multiply,
brown-bottomed tumbling cherubim,
broad-bladed breadfruit leaves
surround his oval virgin
under her ringing sky
the primal vegetation
the mute clangour of lilies,
every brushstroke a prayer
to Giotto, to Masaccio
his primitive, companionable saints.

Never such faith again, never such innocence!

chapter 10

—Frescoes of the New World

The Roman Catholic church at Gros Ilet,
a fat, cream-coloured hunk of masonry,
bluntly concludes the main street of this village
of kneeling shacks, their fences
burdened with violet rosaries, their hinges
rusted from sea-blast.

          The beach
is plagued with flies, at the lime edge
of channel, their black hymn
drones in the ear. The broken paths debouch
onto a broken pier. Before the church
there is a hedge of altar-lace,
a foam-flecked garden whose barefooted path
circles the gabled presbytery
towards a kind of meadow, where a cemetery
rings with the sea. The church is a shell
of tireless silence. The cold vault
cowls like a benediction. There, a young priest,
a Frenchman, Gregorias's friend,
gave him his first commission.

Here was his heaven!
Here was the promise, clear, articulated,
here a new paradise of sea-salt, rum and paint,
sea-wind tempered with turpentine,
his *mundo nuevo*, our new Raphael.
Above the altar-lace
he mounted a triptych of the Assumption
with coarse, purpureal clouds, a prescient Madonna
drawn from Leonardo's "Our Lady of the Rocks."
He soared on his trestles, the curled days shorn
by the adze of Saint Joseph the Worker,
till dusk, the tree of heaven, broke in gold leaf.

Not salt, but his own sorrow sprinkled those
hard-knuckled yards where thorn
trees starved
like their bent nurturers who fed
on the priest's sprinkling hand, whose coarse
mud-crusted feet were yams, whose loss
grew its own roots; O that his art
could sink in earth, as fragrant as Christ's tomb!
But darkness hid
never departing wholly as it promised
between the yam leaves on the river bank
on whose bent heads the rain splintered like mercury,
in shacks like paper lanterns, in green lagoons
whose fading eye held Eden like a transfer,
it hid in yellowing coconuts where the sea-swifts
breaking and forming in their corolla
fluttered like midges round the glare
of the gas lantern. Shadows left the wall, bats
ferried his thoughts across the feverish creek

where the kingfisher startled like a match,
and rows of trees like savages stepped back
from the gas lantern's radiance, from his faith.

Night—and ocean's hiss
enters the lantern. His mind
beds in its nest of snakes.
Over the village the dim stars smelt of sulphur.
They peered through cloth like children with weak eyes
at his life passing.
Like any priest he knew
the darkness of that life was gathering
like oil in the cruses of husked shells,
and that his gift, not he, had made its choice.

ii

Gregorias laughs, a white roar ringed with lamplight,
gigantic moths, the shadows of his hands
fluttering the wall, it is his usual
gesture now, the crucifix.
"Man I ent care if they misunderstand me,
I drink my rum, I praise my God, I mind my business!
The thing is you love death and I love life."
Then, wiping the oracular moustache:
"Your poetry too full of spiders,
bones, worms, ants, things eating up each other,
I can't read it. Look!"
He frames a seascape in a chair,
then, striding back, beyond a table littered
with broken loaves, fishbones, a gut-rusting wine,
he smites his forehead.

64

"Ah, Gregorias, you are a genius, yes!
Yes, God and me, we understand each other." ˙
He hoists his youngest seascape like a child,
kisses, cradles it, opens the window
of the village night, head tilted seaward,
grey gaze serenely clamped,
lean fingers waving, "Listen!"
As if the thunderous Atlantic
were a record he had just put on.
"Listen! Vasco da Gama kneels to the New World."

O Paradiso! sang
the pied shoal at the edge of Half-Moon Battery
netted in sunlight,
swayed in the wash
as the spent swell broke backward.

And it all sang,
surpliced, processional,
the waves clapped their hands, hallelujah!
and the hills were joyful together,
arpeggios of lizards scuttled the leaves,
swift notes, and under earth
the stifled overtures of cannon thunder.

The promontory was hived
with history, tunnels, moss-grimed abandoned armouries.
Across the blue harbour, past the Hospital,
a parched and stubbled headland
like a lion's knuckled paw of tawny grass,
lay the Insane Asylum.
A peel of lemon sand

curled like a rind across the bay's blue dish.
He had his madness,
mine was our history.

iii

O oceanic past,
we were like children
emptying the Atlantic with an enamel cup.
I crouched under each crest
the sneering wave,
the stately foam's *perruque*,
I prayed for it to go
under the fisherman's heel,
for the clods to break
in epochs, crumbling Albion
in each unshelving scarp,
Sidon and Tyre,
an undersea museum,
I saw in the glazed, rocking shallows
the sea-wrack of submerged Byzantium,
as the eddies pushed their garbage to this shore.

Crouched there,
like a whelk-picker,
I searched the sea-wrack for a sea-coin:
my white grandfather's face,
I heard in the black howl of cannon,
sea-agape,
my black grandfather's voice,
and envied mad, divine Gregorias
imprisoned in his choice.

iv

But I tired of your whining, grandfather,
in the whispers of marsh grass,
I tired of your groans, grandfather,
in the deep ground bass of the combers,
I cursed what the elm remembers,
I hoped for your sea-voices
to hiss from my hand,
for the sea to erase
those names a thin,
tortured child, kneeling, wrote
on his slate of wet sand.

chapter **11**

In one house where I went
on irritable sewing errands for my mother,
there was a large tapestry of, was it Waterloo?
a classically chaotic canvas
of snorting, dappled chargers,
their fetlocks folded under swollen bellies,
their nostrils dragonish, smoking,
the bursting marbled eyes elate with fear.
Their riders were a legion of dragoons
sabre-moustached, canted on stiffened rein,
their arms crooked in a scything sweep,
vaulting a heap of dying,
one in the stance of a reclining Venus,
as casual as Giorgione,
surrendering the standard to a sergeant
bent low and gamy as a polo player,
the whole charge like a pukkha, without blood;
in the tainted, cry-haunted fog,
in the grey, flickering mist,
no mouth of pain,
every chivalric wound
rose-lipped, dandiacal, sweet,
every self-sacrifice perfumed;

my head roared with gold.
I bled for all. I thought it full of glory.

Cramming halfheartedly for the Scholarship,
I looked up from my red-jacketed Williamson's
History of the British Empire, towards
the barracks' plumed, imperial hillsides
where cannon-bursts of bamboo sprayed the ridge,
riding to Khartoum, Rorke's Drift,
through dervishes of dust,
behind the chevroned jalousies
I butchered fellaheen, thuggees, Mamelukes, wogs.

Up, past the chrome-green, chalet-sheltering Morne,
where, somebody, possibly Bryan Edwards, wrote:
"Five governors died of yellow fever in that pavilion,"
were the brick barracks. Graves medalled
by pellets of sheepdung, and
the stone curd of the Carib's pothound. Coral.
Tranced at my desk,
groggy with dates, I leant
across my musket. Redcoat ruminant.

    ii

Furred heat prickles this redcoat. Its buttons scorch.
Pellets of salt sweat sting my eyes, once blue,
but which in this green furnace are holes drilled through
by the sun's poker. My bones crack like a torch.
The Fifth stews in its billet behind bounding arches,
the muskets are coolest in their dark, greased armoury,

but our scouts drop like bats. These jungle marches
sickle us, parch us like madmen for a sea
so blue it stains. Downhill a black pig squeals.
Smoke climbs, leisure of recollection.
This forest keeps no wounds, this nature heals
the newest scar, each cloud wraps like a bandage
whatever we enact. What? Chivalry. The fiction
of rusted soldiers fallen on a schoolboy's page.

iii

I saw history through the sea-washed eyes
of our choleric, ginger-haired headmaster,
beak like an inflamed hawk's,
a lonely Englishman who loved parades,
sailing and Conrad's prose.
When the war came the mouths began to bleed,
the white wounds put out tongues.

Nostalgia! Hymns of battles not our own,
on which our fathers looked with the black, iron mouths
of cannon, sea-agape,
to the bugle-coloured light crying from the West,
those dates we piped of redoubt and repulse,
while in our wrists the kettle drums pulsed on
to Khartoum, Lucknow, Cawnpore, Balaclava.
"How strange," said Bill (Carr),
"to find the flag of my regiment,"
where on the razorback ridge
the flag of the Inniskillings every sunset
is hung to bleed for an hour.
A history of ennui, defence, disease,

tumuli of red soldier crabs
that calcified in heaps, their carapaces
freckled with yellow fever,
until the Morne hummed like a hospital,
the gold helmets of dragoons like flowers
tumbling down blue crevasses
in this "Gibraltar of the Gulf of Mexico,"
and on the slate-grey graves more
flowers, medalling their breasts, too late,
fade, "like the white plumes of the Fighting Fifth
who wore the feather without stain."

The leaping Caribs whiten,
in one flash, the instant
the race leapt at Sauteurs,
a cataract! One scream of bounding lace.

      iv

I am pounding the faces of gods back into the red clay they
leapt from with the mattock of heel after heel as if heel
after heel were my thumbs that once gouged out as sacred
vessels for women the sockets of eyes, the deaf howl
of their mouths and I have wept less for them dead than I did
when they leapt from my thumbs into birth, than my
heels which have never hurt horses that now pound them
back into what they should never have sprung from,
staying un-named and un-praised where I found them—
in the god-breeding, god-devouring earth!

We are ground as the hooves of their horses open the wound
of those widening cliffs and the horns of green branches come

lowering past me and the sea's crazed horses the foam
of their whinnying mouths and white mane and the pelting red
pepper of flowers that make my eyes water, yet who am I, under
such thunder, dear gods, under the heels of the thousand
racing towards the exclamation of their single name,
Sauteurs! Their leap into the light? I am no more
than that lithe dreaming runner beside me, my son, the roar
of his heart, and their hearts, I am one with this engine
which is greater than victory, and their pride
with its bounty of pardon, I am one
with the thousand runners who will break on loud sand
at Thermopylae, one wave that now cresting must bear
down the torch of this race, I am all, I am one
who feels as he falls with the thousand now his tendons harden
and the wind-god, Hourucan, combing his hair . . .

      v

In the child's mind
dead fellaheen were heaped in piles of laundry,
and the converted starched with light and sweetness,
white angels flocking round Gordon's golden palms,
the nodding plumes, I SERVE,
resurrected horsemen choiring from the horizon
from the sepia washes of the *Illustrated London News*,
and the child, like a ribbed mongrel
trailing the fading legions,
singing in his grandfather's company.
Peccavi. I have Sind.

Pronounce it. Peace.
Peace to the Fighting Fifth

that wore the feather without stain,
peace to the flutes of bone-shard
and the harvest scythed by fever,
as twilight lowers its lances
against the breastplates of the bole
in quivering shafts, as
night pivots on a sea-gull's rusted winch.
Deep in the trees a glow-worm army haunts
with haunted eyes, their mouths
as soft as moths crying for their lost countries,
translucent yeomanry.
It was their lost blood that rose in her cheek,
their broken buckles which flashed in her hair.

chapter 12

I watched the vowels curl from the tongue of the carpenter's plane,
resinous, fragrant
labials of our forests,
over the plain wood
the back crouched,
the vine-muscled wrist,
like a man rowing,
sweat-fleck on blond cedar.
Disgruntled Dominic.
I sauntered from his dark shop up the Chaussee.

It was still Paris.
                    The twenties. Montparnasse.
Paris, and now its crepuscule
sets in Pound's eye, now as I watch
this twinkling hoar-frost photograph
of the silvery old man bundled, silent, ice-glint
of frozen fire before the enemy,
faites vos hommages,
as the tongues of shavings coil from the moving pen,
to a Paris of plane trees,
to the peeled ease of Hemingway's early prose,
faites vos hommages,
to the hills stippled with violet
as if they had seen Pissarro.

The smell of our own speech,
the smell of baking bread
of drizzled asphalt, this
odorous cedar. After the rain
the rinsed shingles shone,
resinous as the smell of country sweat,
of salt-crusted fishermen.
Christ, to shake off the cerecloths,
to stride from the magnetic sphere of legends,
from the gigantic myth.
To change the marble sweat which pebbled
the wave-blow of stone brows
for this sweat-drop on the cedar plank,
for a future without heroes,
to make out of these foresters and fishermen
heraldic men!

Sunset and dawn like manacles chafed his wrist,
no day broke without chains,
bent like a carpenter over the new wood
a galley-slave over his scarred desk,
hours breaking over his head in paper,
even in his sleep, his hands
like lolling oars.
Where else to row, but backward?
Beyond origins, to the whale's wash,
to the epicanthic Arawak's Hewanora,
back to the impeachable pastoral,
praying the salt scales would flake from our eyes
for a horned, sea-snoring island
barnacled with madrepore,
without the shafts of palms stuck in her side.

Santa Lucia,
patroness of Naples, they had put out her eyes,
saint of the blind,
whose vision was miraculously restored.

The sun came through our skins,
and we beheld, at last,
the exact, sudden definition
of our shadow.
Under our grinding heel
the island burst to a crushed
odour of hogplums, acrid, exuding
a memory stronger than madeleines;
a bay became a blow
from a burnished forehead,
the sea's grin stupefied,
painter and poet walked
the hot road, history-less.

Dating like Christmas cards,
the poinsettia bled deep
into the year, so bright
you expected blood drops on the grass,
next was the season
of the swamp tree's fire,
the foothills blue as smoke,
it was our real, our false
spring. Beside the road,
a beautiful, brown Indian
girl in rags. Sheaves
of brown rice held in brown,
brittle hands, watching us
with that earth-deep darkness

in her gaze. She was
the new Persephone,
dazed, ignorant,
waiting to be named.

ii

But we were orphans of the nineteenth century,
sedulous to the morals of a style,
we lived by another light,
Victoria's orphans, bats in the banyan boughs.
Dragonfly, dragonfly
over that gilded river
like tea-time afternoons with the Old Masters,
in those long pastoral twilights after the War,
dragonfly, your angry vans of gauze
caught in "the light that Samuel Palmer engraved,"
burnt black in the lamp of Giorgione,
dragonfly, in our ears
sang Baudelaire's exhortation to stay drunk,
sang Gauguin's style, awarded Vincent's ear.

I had entered the house of literature as a houseboy,
filched as the slum child stole,
as the young slave appropriated
those heirlooms temptingly left
with the Victorian homilies of *Noli tangere.*
This is my body. Drink.
This is my wine.
Gregorias squeezing the rum-coloured river
with dead limes. Well,
in the beginning, all
drunkenness is Dionysiac, divine.

iii

We drank for all our fathers,
for freedom, as for mine,
how Mama'd praise that angular abstinence,
as if that prim-pursed mouth instantly clicked
at the thought of a quick one,
"Your father never drank,"
self-righteous sphincter!
Starved, burning child,
remember "The Hay Wain"
in your museum, Thomas Craven's book?
The time was coming then,
to your parched mind,
in love with amber, with another light
in the unheard, creaking axle,
the marble-coloured horse
and the charnel harvest-cart,
in the fire-coloured hole eating the woods,
when on the groaning wagon,
the grown mind would sing
"No cure, no cure."

Yet, Gregorias, lit,
we were the light of the world!

iv

And how could we know then,
damned poet and damned painter,
that we too would resemble

those nervous, inflamed men,
fisherman and joiner,
with their quivering addiction
to alcohol and failure,
who hover in a fiction
of flaming palely at doors
for the rumshop lamp to glare,
with watered eyes, loose collars
and the badge of a bone stud,
their vision branched with blood,
their bodies trees which fed
a fire beyond control,
drinkers who lost their pride
when pride in drink was lost.
We saw, within their eyes,
we thought, an artist's ghost,
but dignified, dignified
through days eaten with shame;
we were burned out that year
with the old sacred flame,
we swore to make drink
and art our finishing school,
join brush and pen and name
to the joiner's strenuous tool.

And then, one night, somewhere,
a single outcry rocketed in air,
the thick tongue of a fallen, drunken lamp
licked at its alcohol ringing the floor,
and with the fierce rush of a furnace door
suddenly opened, history was here.

three

A Simple Flame

All have actually parted from the house, but
all truly have remained. And it's not the memory
of them that remains, but they themselves. Nor is
it that they remain in the house but that they
continue because of the house. The functions and
the acts go from the house by train or by plane
or on horseback, walking or crawling. What continues
in the house is the organ, the gerundial or circular
agent. The steps, the kisses, the pardons, the crimes
have gone. What continues in the house is the foot,
the lips, the eyes, the heart. Negations and affir-
mations, good and evil have scattered. What continues
in the house is the subject of the act.

Cesar Vallejo
Poemas Humanos

chapter 13

The whole sky caught. The thick sea heaved like petrol.
The past hissed in a cinder.
They heard the century breaking in half.
Then, towards daybreak, rain
sprinkled the cinders. Clouds
steamed from the broken axle-tree.

The sky, vibrating, rippled like sheet iron,
like hairy behemoths, their lungs burnt out, the hills
were hoarse with smoke, everywhere
the retching odours of a tannery.
Clouds curled like burnt-out papers at their edges,
the telephone wires sang from pole to pole
parodying perspective. The wall of heat,
now menacing, now a thief giving ground,
stepped back with every step,
the sea was level with the street.
Every lot of desolation stood
absurdly walled, its toothless breach confessing
perverted bedsprings, heat-stained mattresses,
all of the melancholy, monotonous rubbish
of those who thought their lives strange to their neighbours,
their sins repeated tiredly by the same
picture-frames, papers, blue magnesia bottles,

under arched, amnesiac stairways,
hesitating:

      Soon, on the promontory,
an atmosphere resembling what they had read of war
began its bivouac fires, haphazard tents,
lives casually tangled like unsorted laundry.
Then, like rifle-fire, the flutes of smoke,
the first, white flags of washing,
were bravely signalling that some pact
of common desolation had begun.
In the ruins, a population of ragpickers,
bent over stones, deciphering their graves.
Hoses plied the shambles
making the ashes mud.
Here were the broken arches and the vines
ascending leisurely, with the languor of fire.
Your ruined Ilion, your grandfather's pyre.

    ii

A landscape of burnt stones and broken arches
arranged itself with a baroque panache.
On somnolent, townless twilights, when
piano practice sprinkled the dyed air
before the grid of stars budded with lights
above a system of extinguished streets
he headed for the promontory across the harbour,
from the old town to where in the old barracks
the refugees began another life.
Buckets clanged under the public pipes,
furred dusk clawed softly, mewing at his ear,

all of the sounds of evening fell on velvet,
the night was polishing star after star,
the mild, magnificent night with all its studs on,
buttoned and soldierly, with nowhere to march.
Below the fort, from fields of silver water,
the moon rose on a chiton-fluted sea.

iii

Perched on the low stern of the rented shallop,
he watched the barracks on the hill dilate
with every stroke behind the oarsman's ear.
The rower, silent, kept his gaze oblique-
ly fixed on the wharf's receding beacon,
a mannequin with a skirt of lacy iron, and
in the opaque, slowly-colouring harbour
the one sound was the plump plash of the oars,
each stroke concluding with the folded gurgle
of an intaken breath. Weakly protesting,
the oarlock's squeak, the gunwale's heaving lurch,
the pause upheld after each finished stroke,
unstudied, easy, pentametrical,
one action, and one thought. Halfway across
the chord between the downstroke of the oar
and its uplifted sigh was deepened
by a donkey's rusty winch, from Foux Lachaud,
a herring-gull's one creak, till the bay grew
too heavy for reflection. The rower veered
precisely, triangulating his approach,
headed for an abandoned rocky inlet
that reeked of butchered turtles, then the shallop
skimmed shallow water, the coast sliding

past easily, easily sliding rocks and trees
over the mossed mosaic of bright stones,
making their arrival secret. He would remember
a child in a canted whaleboat rounding this harbour,
coves chopped in a crescent by the whale's jaw,
with "Boy" or "Babs" Monplaisir at the tiller,
now, lecherous, lecherous, sighed the insucked water,
muttered the wiry writhing sun-shot creeks
and grasses, lecherous, skittered the thin,
translucent minnows from the skiff's shadow,
you with your finger in the pie of sin,
you with an iron in the fire, tell her
that the house could speak. Odour of fish,
odour of lechery. Who spoke? I,
said the Indian woman you finger-poked in the doorway.

I, said the Negro whore on the drawing-room floor
under the silent portraits of your parents,
while Anna slept,
her golden body like a lamp blown out
that holds, just blown, the image of the flame.

iv

Magical lagoon, stunned
by its own reflection!
The boat, the stone
pier, the water-odorous
boathouse, the trees
so quiet they were always
far. I could drown there,

86

as now, even now, an Ann,
Anna, Andreuille,
swims from a ring of whispering
young sisters, her head
emerging from their
swirling eddy.

The sixteen-year-old sun
plates her with light,
freckled, from now on
her colour only,

leaf-freckled forearm
brown of leafless April,
the russet hair, the freckled
big-boned wrist. Reader,

imagine the boat stayed,
the harbour stayed, the oar's
uplifted wand,

hold the light's changes to
a single light, repeat
the voyage, delay the arrival,
in that bright air,

he wished himself moving
yet forever there.
The disc of the world turned
slowly, she was its centre,

the chill of water entered

the shell of her palm,
in membranous twilight
the match of the first star

through the door of sunset always left ajar.
And all bread savoured
of her sunburnt nape,

her laughter a white napkin
shaken under the leaves.
We sit by the stone wall

all changes to grey stone,
stone hands, stone air,
stone eyes, from which

irisless, we stare,
wishing the sea were stone,
motion we could not hear.

No silence, since,
its equal.

For one late afternoon, when again she stood
in the door of a twilight always left ajar,
when dusk had softened the first bulb
the colour of the first weak star,
I asked her, "Choose,"
the amazed dusk held its breath,
the earth's pulse staggered,
she nodded, and that nod
married earth with lightning.

And now we were the first guests of the earth
and everything stood still for us to name.
Against the blades of palms and yellow sand,
I hear that open laugh,
I see her stride
as ruthless as that flax-bright harvester
Judith, with Holofernes' lantern in her hand.

    v

And a vein opened in the earth,
its drops congealing into plum,
sorrel and berry,
the year bleeding again, Noel, Noel,
blood for the bloodless birth,
blood deepening the poinsettia's Roman blades
after the Festival of the Innocents.
Life changing direction with the Trades.
A fresh wind, irrepressibly elate,
lifted the leaves' skirts, romped
down the Roman balconies,
polishing all that was already polished,
the sky, leaves, metal, and her face.
At nights in the Cantonment,
when the mouth of the full moon sang through the ruins,
choirs of black carollers patrolled the Barracks
singing of holly and fresh-fallen snow,
among them, Anna,
profile of hammered gold,
head by Angelico,
stars choiring in gold leaf.

And Christmas came with its pretence at cold,
apples bubbled in barrows, the wind, beggarly
polished their cheeks;
along smoked kitchen-walls, like a laboratory
sweet, devilish concoctions, knuckles, roots,
blood-jellied jars, pungent and aromatic as the earth
which kept its secret till this season, were fermenting,
bark-knuckled ginger, the crimson bulbs
of sorrel like extinguished lights
packed up in last year's tinsel, sweated oil,
and the baked earth exuded
itself, as if, pebbled with clove,
it could at last be taken from its oven,
the night smelled like a cake
seasoned in anise, Falernum and Madeira,
and the ruby glass of the chapels brimmed with wine.

vi

But this as well; some nights, after he left her,
his lechery like a mongrel nosed the ruins,
past Manoir's warehouse. In her absence
his nostrils prickled for the scent of sea-grapes;
Gregorias would laugh, "Drink, take a next sip.
You are creating this, and it will end.
The world is not like this,
nor is she, friend."

The cold glass was her lip.
Every room he entered was an album
from which her image had been crudely torn.

chapter 14

—Anna awaking

When the oil green water glows but doesn't catch,
only its burnish, something wakes me early,
draws me out breezily to the pebbly shelf
of shallows where the water chuckles
and the ribbed boats sleep like children,
buoyed on their creases. I have nothing to do,
the burnished kettle is already polished,
to see my own blush burn,
and the last thing the breeze needs is my exhilaration.

I lie to my body with useless chores.
The ducks, if they ever slept, waddle knowingly.
The pleats of the shallows are neatly creased
and decorous and processional,
they arrive at our own harbour from the old Hospital
across the harbour. When the first canoe,
silent, will not wave at me,
I understand, we are acknowledging
our separate silences, as the one silence,
I know that they know my peace as I know theirs.
I am amazed that the wind is tirelessly fresh.
The wind is older than the world.

It is always one thing at a time.
Now, it is always girlish.
I am happy enough to see it as a kind
of dimpled, impish smiling.
When the sleep-smelling house stirs
to that hoarse first cough, that child's first cry,
that rumbled, cavernous questioning of my mother,
I come out of the cave
like the wind emerging,
like a bride, to her first morning.

I shall make coffee.
The light, like a fiercer dawn,
will singe the downy edges of my hair,
and the heat will plate my forehead till it shines.
Its sweat will share the excitement of my cunning.
Mother, I am in love.
Harbour, I am waking.
I know the pain in your budding, nippled limes,
I know why your limbs shake, windless, pliant trees.
I shall grow grey as this light.
The first flush will pass.
But there will always be morning,
and I shall have this fever waken me,
whoever I lie to, lying close to, sleeping
like a ribbed boat in the last shallows of night.

But even if I love not him but the world,
and the wonder of the world in him, of him in the world,
and the wonder that he makes the world waken to me,
I shall never grow old in him,
I shall always be morning to him,

and I must walk and be gentle as morning.
Without knowing it, like the wind,
that cannot see her face,
the serene humility of her exultation,
that having straightened the silk sea smooth, having noticed
that the comical ducks ignore her, that
the childish pleats of the shallows are set straight,
that everyone, even the old, sleeps in innocence,
goes in nothing, naked, as I would be,
if I had her nakedness, her transparent body.
The bells garland my head. I could be happy,
just because today is Sunday. No, for more.

ii

Then Sundays, smiling, carried in both hands
a towelled dish bubbling with the good life
whose fervour steaming, beaded her clear brow,
from which damp skeins were brushed,
and ladled out her fullness to the brim.
And all those faded prints that pressed their scent
on her soft, house-warm body,
glowed from her flesh with work,
her hands that held the burnish of dry hillsides
freckled with fire-light,
hours that ripened till the fullest hour
could burst with peace.

"Let's go for a little walk," she said, one afternoon,
"I'm in a walking mood." Near the lagoon,
dark water's lens had made the trees one wood
arranged to frame this pair whose pace

unknowingly measured loss,
each face was set towards its character.
Where they now stood, others before had stood,
the same lens held them, the repeated wood,
then there grew on each one
the self-delighting, self-transfiguring stone
stare of the demi-god.
Stunned by their images they strolled on, content
that the black film of water kept the print
of their locked images when they passed on.

iii

And which of them in time would be betrayed
was never questioned by that poetry
which breathed within the evening naturally,
but by the noble treachery of art
that looks for fear when it is least afraid,
that coldly takes the pulse-beat of the heart
in happiness; that praised its need to die
to the bright candour of the evening sky,
that preferred love to immortality;
so every step increased that subtlety
which hoped that their two bodies could be made
one body of immortal metaphor.
The hand she held already had betrayed
them by its longing for describing her.

chapter 15

Still dreamt of, still missed,
especially on raw, rainy mornings, your face shifts
into anonymous schoolgirl faces, a punishment,
since sometimes, you condescend to smile,
since at the corners of the smile there is forgiveness.

Besieged by sisters, you were a prize
of which they were too proud, circled
by the thorn thicket of their accusation,
what grave deep wrong, what wound have you brought Anna?

The rain season comes with its load.
The half-year has travelled far. Its back hurts.
It drizzles wearily.

It is twenty years since,
after another war, the shell-cases are where?
But in our brassy season, our imitation autumn,
your hair puts out its fire,
your gaze haunts innumerable photographs,

now clear, now indistinct,
all that pursuing generality,
that vengeful conspiracy with nature,

all that sly informing of objects,
and behind every line, your laugh
frozen into a lifeless photograph.

In that hair I could walk through the wheatfields of Russia,
your arms were downed and ripening pears,
for you became, in fact, another country,

you are Anna of the wheatfield and the weir,
you are Anna of the solid winter rain,
Anna of the smoky platform and the cold train,
in that war of absence, Anna of the steaming stations,

gone from the marsh-edge,
from the drizzled shallows
puckering with gooseflesh,
Anna of the first green poems that startingly hardened,

of the mellowing breasts now,
Anna of the lurching, long flamingoes
of the harsh salt lingering in the thimble
of the bather's smile,

Anna of the darkened house, among the reeking shell-cases
lifting my hand and swearing us to her breast,
unbearably clear-eyed.

You are all Annas, enduring all goodbyes,
within the cynical station of your body,
Christie, Karenina, big-boned and passive,

that I found life within some novel's leaves

more real than you, already chosen
as his doomed heroine. You knew, you knew.

ii

Who were you, then?
The golden partisan of my young Revolution,
my braided, practical, seasoned commissar,

your back, bent at its tasks, in the blue kitchen,
or hanging flags of laundry, feeding the farm's chickens,
against a fantasy of birches,

poplars or whatever.
As if a pen's eye could catch that virginal litheness,
as if shade and sunlight leoparding the blank page
could be so literal,

foreign as snow,
far away as first love,
my Akhmatova!

Twenty years later, in the odour of burnt shells,
you can remind me of "A Visit to the Pasternaks,"
so that you are suddenly the word "wheat,"

falling on the ear, against the frozen silence of a weir,
again you are bending
over a cabbage garden, tending
a snowdrift of rabbits,
or pulling down the clouds from the thrumming clotheslines

If dreams are signs,
then something died this minute,
its breath blown from a different life,

from a dream of snow, from paper
to white paper flying, gulls and herons
following this plough. And now,

you are suddenly old, white-haired,
like the herons, the turned page. Anna, I wake
to the knowledge that things sunder
from themselves, like peeling bark,

to the emptiness
of a bright silence shining after thunder.

iii

"Any island would drive you crazy,"
I knew you'd grow tired
of all that iconography of the sea

like the young wind, a bride
riffling daylong the ocean's catalogue
of shells and algae,

everything, this flock
of white, novitiate herons
I saw in the grass of a grey parish church,

like nurses, or young nuns after communion,

their sharp eyes sought me out
as yours once, only.

And you were heron-like,
a water-haunter,
you grew bored with your island,

till, finally, you took off,
without a cry,
a novice in your nurse's uniform,

years later I imagined you
walking through trees to some grey hospital,
serene communicant,
but never "lonely,"

like the wind, never to be married,
your faith like folded linen, a nun's, a nurse's,
why should you read this now?

No woman should read verses
twenty years late. You go about your calling, candle-like
carrying yourself down a dark aisle

of wounded, married to the sick,
knowing one husband, pain,
only with the heron-flock, the rain,

the stone church, I remembered . . .
Besides, the slender, virginal New Year's
just married, like a birch
to a few crystal tears,

99

and like a birch bent at the register
who cannot, for a light's flash, change her name,
she still writes '65 for '66;

so, watching the tacit
ministering herons, each at its
work among the dead, the stone church, the stones,

I made this in your honour, when
vows and affections failing
your soul leapt like a heron sailing
from the salt, island grass

into another heaven.

iv

Anna replies:

I am simple,
I was simpler then.
It was simplicity
which seemed so sensual.

What could I understand,
the world, the light? The light
in the mud-stained sea-wash,
the light in a gull's creak

letting the night in?
They were simple to me,
I was not within them as simply

as I was within you.

It was your selflessness
which loved me as the world,
I was a child, as much
as you, but you brought the tears

of too many contradictions,
I became a metaphor, but
believe me I was unsubtle as salt.

And I answer, Anna,
twenty years after,
a man lives half of life,
the second half is memory,

the first half, hesitation
for what should have happened
but could not, or

what happened with others
when it should not.

A gleam. Her burning grip. The brass shell-cases,
oxidised, the brass reeking of cordite,
forty-one years after the Great War. The gleam
of brass reburnished in the allamanda,
through the barbed wire of bougainvillea thorns
beyond the window, on the sun-chevroned porch
I watched the far cannon-smoke of cloud
above the Morne, wounded, struck-dumb,
as she drew my hand firmly to the firstness

of the crisp, fragile cloth across her breast,
in a locked silence, she the nurse,
I the maimed soldier. There have been
other silences, none as deep. There has since
been possession, none as sure.

chapter 16

—The cement phoenix

Meanwhile to one metre, in the burnt town
things found the memory of their former places,
that vase of roses slowly sought its centre
like a film reeled backward, like
a poltergeist reversed.
Oleographs of Christ the Sacred Heart
sailed towards their new hooks and anchored there,
doilies like feathers floating settled softly,
frames drew their portraits like a closing rose,
laces resumed their spinsterish precision
and parlours were once more varnished, sacrosanct.
Apartment blocks whitened the air,
cul-de-sacs changed their dialect patronyms
to boulevards and avenues,
the cement phoenix rose.
All day in the gutted roads of the new city
the cement mixers snarled American, white-faced
the city entered its half-century.

Slowly she rose, the New Jerusalem
created in the image of *The Commonwealth Today,*
a hearty brochure from Whitehall

showing Welfare Officers grinning behind prize bulls
at county fairs, the new Senior Civil Servant
folded in his greatcoat, the phoenix metaphor flew
from tongue to tongue.
                              New cement blocks
five or six stories high
in their didactic Welfare State severity,
boulevards short of breath
confronted the old town.
From the verandah of the old wooden college
I watched the turning pages of the sea.

I leant across the rakish balcony
smelling the sunlit iron of the burnt town.
Burnt flesh. Our blitz was over too. I felt
the voices of children under my feet.
"Saul has slain his thousand,
David his ten thousand."

The bones of our Hebraic faith were scattered
over such a desert, burnt and brackened gorse,
their war was over, it had not been
the formal tapestry bled white by decorum,
it had infected language,
gloria Dei and the glory of
the Jacobean bible were the same. The shoes
of cherubs piled in pyramids
outside the Aryan ovens.

A ghost, accosting, softly grew beside me.
My other self, the Brother, the mathematical Poet,
scented with mint, he cited, softly, Perse:

"The beauty of this world hath made me sad."
I turned and studied him. Our smiles blent.
He possessed the bulging, tubercular stare,
the shadow-sooted eyes whose sockets held the hunger
of survivors of the death-camps and the soap-vats,
but, bony, muscular as his body was
and thinly sheeted with its film of sweat
it hinted of deeper emaciation,
a gnawing, lacerated elegance.
The Andrew Aguecheek hair thinned like flax
winnowed from the bumpy skull, a phrenologist's field-day,
so wispy-frail, so oven-singed,
you feared the lightest breeze would sear him bald.
He, too, a poet once. His, too, this exile!
Never to leave his isle, till Mary called him,
to sit and watch the twilight in this harbour
igniting other lives, watching the herring-gulls rehearse
with every dusk their cycles of departure,
to watch the visionary glare
tarnish to tin. To hear, waking at night,
the rain driving its nails into this ground,
into his hands, to walk the kelp-piled beach
and hear the waves arriving with stale news.
Go then, I thought, but the wave held back my hand,
the grass felt hurt, the stars shone without privilege,
in those soft dusks, like him,
it rained within me as it rained on Ireland.

While, in the dark hold below the coffin-planks,
a generation of slaves' children sang
"Where balmy breezes blow
Soft winds are playing . . .

105

Santaaa Lucheeeea
Santaaa Lucheeeea."
Steered now by Irish hands to their new epoch.

Other men's voices,
other men's lives and lines.

The accolade, the accolade.
Tea with the British Council Representative,
tannin, calfskin, gilt and thank you vellum much,
of course you will soon shed your influences,
silvery cadence measured, the eavesdropping coarse vegetation
outside white jalousies, the indoor palms
nodding to Mr. Winters's approbation,
a rubicund, gurgling consul, "keener on music"
but capable of knowing talent when he sees it.
I am hoisted on silvery chords upward,
eager for the dropped names like sugar cubes.
Eliot. Plop. Benjamin Britten. Klunk. Elgar. Slurp.
Mrs. Winters's cheeks gleaming. Polished cherries.
Lawns. Elegance. Remembering elms. England, then. When?
Down on her speckled forearm. More tea.
Thank you my mind burrowing her soft scented crotch.
First intimations of immortality.
Other men's wives.

ii

Sister Annunziata
sat by the white wall
of the convent balcony
whose shadows alternated

like the piano keys
of her pupil's practice,
under its black snood
her starched brow, a wall
of ageing ivory,
listened as Anna played
in the rivering afternoon,
arpeggios of minnows
widening from her hand,
as through the chapel prism
Sister Gabriela
settled like a tired pigeon,
old nun whose steel glasses
flashed spears into her Christ,
Annunziata's head
a wall of virgin plaster
below which her dark eyes
burned fiercely in their niche.

And to the monody of piano practice
gables looped the skyline of the old town,
swifts scored the air,
jalousies shuttered like the singer's eyes,
but in those idling afternoons
the one melody more sorrowful
than some frail Irish air
was the old theme of smoke rising from back yards
barred with rusted tin, the thin
search for something that had surrendered soon.

I walked down to the wharf, as usual
looking seaward,

the island lowered
the sun, and rocked
slowly, at anchor.
The usual smoky twilight
blackened our galvanised roof with its nail-holes of stars,
the old dark tarred the wharves,
the mesmerised dogfishes glared
through phosphorus and the stunned eels wriggled
in the ochre arclight of Prince Albert's Basin,
where the schooners smelt of islands,
and far out, the fireflies
or villas signalled an incoming liner
far as Christmas.
Earth-heart, I prayed,
nerves of raw fibre,
uproot me, yet
let what I have sworn to love not feel betrayed
when I must go, and, if I must go,
make of my heart an ark
let my ribs bear
all, doubled by
memory, down to the emerald fly
marrying this hand, and be
the image of a young man on a pier
his heart a ship within a
ship within a ship, a bottle
where this wharf, these
rotting roofs, this sea,
sail, sealed in glass.

iii

To that vow were addressed all those vibrations of rain
like a railing echoing arpeggios where her fingers
sounded, as the day bending gathered
the fallen clouds before nightfall;
they were shaping their fallacy
in your breast, like an ancient engraving
of Italianate cabbage palms, where the feathery leaves
of flamboyants backed the old landscapes.
How often didn't you hesitate
between rose-flesh and sepia,
your blood like a serpent whispering
of a race incapable of subtler shadow,
of music, architecture and a complex thought.
In that acid was evening etched,
a coppery glaze plated the landscape
till your envious anger accused it of being too poor;
but be glad that you were touched
by some other's sadness, that when your hand trembles
and the tightening railings sound,
or the sky, before rain, sounds like a monstrous shell
where their voices are, be happy
in every uncertainty. Cherish the stumbling
that lashes your eyes with branches,
that, threatened with rain,
your sorrow is still uncertain.

You had begun to write those letters to no one,
your friends, like leaves, seemed too preoccupied
with balance. You faced the blank page

and trembled, you had learnt by heart
the monotonous scrawl of the beaches
for years trying to reach you,
delivering the same message, Go,
in the crab's carapace from which the crabsoul had vanished,
in eyes ground the colour of sea-stone.
Their lives slipped into your own
like letters under a door.

chapter 17

Note after note the year was orchestrating
those wires of manuscript ruled on its clouds
till they were black with swallows quavering
for their surge north. Lightning frequently
crackled across the watersheds, thunder
rattled the sky's tightened parchment.
He haunted beaches,
the horizon tightened round his throat.
Their wings flashing like tinfoil
the sanderlings refused his messages.
The islands were a string of barges towed nowhere,
every view
assembling itself to say farewell.

At Vieuxfort
the soldiers had broken up their base and gone,
the mustard-yellow bungalows through the palms
were empty or dismantled. Behind the tarred screens,
behind the rusting fly-wire, nothing stirred,
the runways cracked open like an idiot's smile.

The steady salt air
from the open Atlantic rusted bolts,
air hangars, latches, children's toys,

the wooden treaders gave, grey, plump with rot.
From Micoud to L'Anse Paradis
the breakers, like a louder silence, roared.

ii

There were ducks, supposedly,
that used the windward coast as a way station
on their haul south from as far as Sombreor
and La Isla de Pinos to Brazil.
I looked for them flying, stupidly, at daybreak,
I felt the instinct of their passage,
but I saw none.
                    The only birds
were the pernickety, finical sanderlings,
their coats turned white for winter,
testing the shallows' edge,
their parallels as far as the wild ducks.
And still I saw
the possibility of angels,
suction of their bare heel razed from the sand,
in the wind-chased brightness after their shadows
raced from the tide, their flight followed so often
by the look-they-have-left-us impulse of sanderlings
over bright water, and herring-gulls circled
the eddy where heaven had sucked them in,
I knew where they hid behind the walls of cloud,
I heard when they rushed from bent canes urgently
to bless some other island, I was the guest
of their impatient presence, one voice behind
my father's, one foot impressed in
the sand-indenting heel of a seraph,

I saw their colour,
in the steel, silver scales of the sea,
rasp-winged and hoarse in their fretful, marshalled flocks,
work-worn and restless, and when they turned
their gaze, it was not the glare of eagles,
they were not eternity's falcons,
but impatient, commissioned beings, their fierce
expressionless look benign and tolerant,
they were simple as gulls
not caring if they were noticed,
when we were gone, others
would watch them.
They were without revenge,
for those who left them
their only punishment was absence.

iii

And so one summer after I returned, we arranged
to stay in the old village and we spent
two days and one night there, but except
for the first few hours it was somehow different,
as if either the island or myself had changed,
but not Gregorias, and we both spent
a bad night sleeping on our shoes for pillows,
hearing the rasping surf until the dawn,
but it was not the same at dawn, it was a book
you'd read a life ago walking up the brown
sand, the filth, and where the sea breaks at La Vierge,
a dead mind wandering at the long billows,
and I left there that morning with a last look
at things that would not say what they once meant.

One dawn the sky was warm pink thinning to no colour.
In it, above the Morne, the last star shone
measuring the island with its callipers.
As usual, everywhere, the sinuations of cockcrow,
a leisured, rusting, rising and falling,
echoed the mountain line. The day creaked
wearily open. A wash of meagre blue entered the sky.
The final star diminished and withdrew.
Day pivoted on a sea-gull's screeching hinge.
And the year closed. The allamandas fell,
medalling the shoulders of the last visitor.
At the airport, I looked towards the beach.
The sand had seen battalions come and go,
the vines had written their memorials,
all of that cannonfire taken up by cloud.
Nothing had altered the teal or mallard's route,
all that salt blood thinned out in the salt surf.
I shook Gregorias's hand. Dead almond leaf.
There was no history. No memory.
Rocks haunted by sea-birds, that was all.
The house would survive, my brother would survive,
and yet how arrogant, how cruel
to think the island and Anna would survive
(since they were one), inviolate, under
their sacred and inverted bell of glass,
and that I was incapable of betrayal,
to imagine their lives revolving round my future,
to accept as natural their selfless surrender.
The three faces I had most dearly loved

that year, among the blurred faces in the crowd,
Gregorias laughing, "Jamaica just up the road, man,
just up the road." Harry hustling. Anna had not moved.
I watched the island narrowing, the fine
writing of foam around the precipices, then
the roads as small and casual as twine
thrown on its mountains, I watched till the plane
turned to the final north and turned above
the open channel with the grey sea between
the fishermen's islets until all that I love
folded in cloud. I watched the shallow green
breaking in places where there would be reef,
the silver glinting on the fuselage, each mile
tightening us and all fidelity strained
till space would snap it. Then, after a while
I thought of nothing, nothing, I prayed, would change.
When we set down at Seawell it had rained.

No metaphor, no metamorphosis,
as the charcoal-burner turns
into his door of smoke,
three lives dissolve in the imagination,
three loves, art, love and death,
fade from a mirror clouding with this breath,
not one is real, they cannot live or die,
they all exist, they never have existed:

Harry, Dunstan, Andreuille.

four

The Estranging Sea

Who order'd that their longing's fire
Should be, as soon as kindled, cool'd?
Who renders vain their deep desire?—
A God, a God their severance ruled!
And bade betwixt their shores to be
The unplumb'd, salt, estranging sea.

Arnold
To Marguerite

chapter 18

—Noa Noa

You can't beat brushing young things from the country
in the country self. Might wind up there myself.
Black lissome limbs and teeth like fresh-cooked yams,
backs smooth and sleek like rainwashed aubergines
and tits like nippled naseberries, and he did that,
Gauguin had gone, Harry had built his mansion
upon the beached verge of the salt flood,
within a sea of roaring leaves, the gales
driving his houseboat deeper in the forest, buoyed
by green breakers of ocean the long night,
he had blacked out for their millennium,
a clock too tired to tell the time,
he had exchanged their future for the prime
simplicities of salt pork seasoning the pot,
for the white rum growling in his gut for lunch,
the smell of baked earth rising from the grid
of noon, for the cloud-cloth steaming in the tin
where the scale-backed breadfruit gurgled like a turtle
for another life, for jahbal and vahine.
Telling himself that although it stank
this was the vegetable excrement of natural life,
not their homogenised, chemical-ridden shit,
that there on the leafy ocean with his saints,

Vincent and Paul, his yellowing *Letters to Theo*
and *Noa Noa*, though the worms bored their gospel,
he no longer wanted what he could become,
his flame, made through their suffering, their flame,
nightly by the brass-haloed lamp, he prayed
whatever would come, come.

                                 Why not, indeed? In deed.
There was his hand and the shadow of his hand,
there was his thought and the shadow of that thought
lying lighter than the shadow of a sound
across coarse canvas or the staring paper,
the quiet panic at the racing sun
his breath held before its trembling wick,
the done with its own horror of the undone
that frays us all to pieces and breakdown,
all of us, always, all ways, one after one.

He faced the canvas, bored
with the downseamed face of a man used
to giving orders, but before he began
the surface would acquire its old ambition.
It could not understand this newer life.
A spider began to thread
easel to bedstead.

                  Now, where he had beheld
a community of graceful spirits
irradiating from his own control and centre,
through botany, history, lepidoptery, stamps,
his mind was cracking like the friable earth,
and in each chasm,
sprung nettles like the hands of certain friendships.

Sunset grew blacker in the fisherman's flesh.
He would resolve into a fish unless he left
the long beach darkening, for the village lamps,
with the claws of the furred sea gripping the high ground,
his eyes would phosphoresce, his head
bubble with legends through the fly-like heads
of fishnets slung between the poles,
where the palm trees were huge spiders stuck on shafts.
Fear rooted him. Run, like a child again, run, run!
The morning bleeds itself away,
everything he touches breaks,
like a child again, he reads
the legend of Midas and the golden touch,
from morning through the afternoon
he feels compelled to read
the enormous and fragile literature
of breakdown. It is like that visit
to that trembling girl, at whose quivering side,
her skin like a plagued foal's,
my own compassion quivered,
dark moons moving under her glazed eyelids,
who answers, "How was it?
It was all trembling."
It is fear and trembling.

      ii

Its initial intimation is
indifference to the uncontrollable,
to ease into the terrifying spaces
like Pascal's bloated body pricked out with stars,
to see, swimming towards us,

121

the enormous, lidless eyeball of the moon,
dumb, gibbering with silence, struck
by something it cannot answer
or the worst, the worst, an oceanic nothing,
it is all trembling,
it is fear and trembling.
It is the uncontrollable
persistence of the heartbeat,
the sweat, the twitching eye,
the hand from which the brush slips on its own,
the finical signals of an overdue defeat,
to tire of life, and yet not wish to die.

And yet, and yet,
the same day will persist in being good,
either its nature has not learnt to forget,
or fear was a faith it never understood;
it hoisted, stubbornly, its yards and spinnakers,
believed immortally in blue,
and had, as usual, the old engine, love,
nodded acknowledgement to the supreme maker's
hand, yet could not tell you why, or how it moved,
its bow of daylight driving to the dark,
as if its love,
and the stunned blue afternoon were life enough.

iii

Irascibility, muse of middle age.
How often you have felt you have wasted your life
among a people with no moral centre,
to want to move from the contagion of too many friends,

the heart congealing into stone,
how many would prefer to this poem
to see you drunken in a gutter,
and to catch in the corner of their workrooms
the uncertified odour of your death?
And perhaps, master, you saw early
what brotherhood means among the spawn of slaves
hassling for return trips on the middle passage,
spitting on their own poets,
preferring their painters drunkards,
for their solemn catalogue of suicides,
as I draw nearer your desolation, Cesar Vallejo,
and its raining Thursdays.

Do not tell me the world is the same,
that life is hard as a stone,
for I have known it when it was a flower
potent, annihilating with promise.
That the worst of us are wolves.
I no longer care for whom I write,
as you found in your hand, sir,
that terrible paralysis of their vindication
that out of such a man,
nothing would come,
they said that, and were already composing,
some by a sentence, some by a phrase, some by their spit,
but most with a dry remark, like a fistful of dirt
flung into your grave, from such a man
what would you expect,
but a couple of paintings
and a dog's life?

I would refrain,
I withhold from myself that curse,
but in this battle, it is them, or me,
and as it was you who lost,
and they who pitied your losing,
and they who deny now their victory,
it is, it is sad, though, a struggle,
without engagement.

iv

Let this one remember how
I closed with gentleness,
as if I were his brother,
with all the love that I had left
his sister's young eyes,
and the same one, the *chauve*-head
with the harelip and the lisp
that is, if I had only known, a serpent's,
certain matters of money,
certain matters of preferment,
and so many other embarrassments,
but I need to write them,
or I myself would not believe
that the world has left such men,
that the race is still a stigma,
that the truth is nothing more
than a puddle of clear water
dammed in a ditch. Still, master, I cannot
enter the inertia of silence.
My hands, like those of a madman's,

cannot be tied. I have no friends
but the oldest, words. This, at least,
master, none can take from me.
But the path increases with snakes.

No,
think of the weight which
the delicate blades of the fern endure,
the weight of the world, and
everything else in its world that is not
fern, yet it can be eased from
earth by a fist, rainstorms richen its
roots, what it takes from wind
is hard to believe, but its sweat
gleams, it is chained in its own dew,
it is locked into earth, unlike the delicate
ribs of some men. Uprooted
they quail.

For here, what was success?
It was the mean, inner
excitement at having survived.
Had he been freed? Or
had heart, guts and talent
exhausted him? Every muscle
ached like a rusting hawser
to hoist him heavenward towards
his name, pierced with the stars
of Raphael, Saint Greco, and later,
not stars, but the people's medals,
with Siqueiros, Gauguin, Orozco,
Saint Vincent and Saint Paul.
It would be worth it to fall,

with the meteor's orange brushstroke
from a falling hand, to hope
there is painting in heaven.

The Muse of inanition, the dead nerve,
where was the world in which we felt the centre,
our *mundo nuevo*, handed to black hands
copying the old laws, the new mistakes? Where?
Speak to the Indian grazing his two cows
across the allotment.

"The brown one now [the cow], she is in season,
she was calling last moon."
"Why you don't ask the government for a farm?"
"Well, I apply, but all dem big boys so, dem ministers,
dem have their side. Cockroach must step aside
to give fowl chance." Ah, brave third world!

Cockroach must step aside to give fowl chance.
Leaves of the long afternoon silverly trembling.

chapter 19

—Frescoes of the New World II

My Anna, my Beatrice,
I enclose in this circle of hell,
in the stench of their own sulphur of self-hatred,
in the steaming, scabrous rocks of Soufrière,
in the boiling, pustular volcanoes of the South,
all o' dem big boys, so, dem ministers,
ministers of culture, ministers of development,
the green blacks, and their old toms,
and all the syntactical apologists of the Third World
explaining why their artists die,
by their own hands, magicians of the New Vision.
Screaming the same shit.
Those who peel, from their own leprous flesh, their names,
who chafe and nurture the scars of rusted chains,
like primates favouring scabs, those who charge tickets
for another free ride on the middle-passage,
those who explain to the peasant why he is African,
their catamites and eunuchs banging tambourines,
whores with slave-bangles banging tambourines,
and the academics crouched like rats
listening to tambourines
jackals and rodents feathering their holes

hoarding the sea-glass of their ancestors' eyes,
sea-lice, sea-parasites on the ancestral sea-wrack,
whose god is history. *Pax.*
Who want a new art,
and their artists dying in the old way.
Those whose promises drip from their mouths like pus.
Geryons gnawing their own children.
These are the dividers,
they encompass our history,
in their hands is the body
of my friend and the future,
they measure the skulls with callipers
and pronounce their measure
of toms, of traitors, of traditionals and AfroSaxons.
They measure them carefully
as others once measured the teeth
of men and horses, they measure and divide.
Their music comes from the rattle of coral bones,
their eyes like worms drill into parchments,
they measure each other's sores
to boast who has suffered most,
and their artists keep dying,
they are the saints of self-torture,
their stars are pimples of pus
on the night of our grandfathers,
they are hired like dogs to lick the sores of their people,
their vision blurs, their future is clouded with cataract,
but out of its mist, one man,
whom they will not recognise, emerges
and staggers towards his lineaments.

chapter 20

> *—Down their carved names*
> *the raindrop ploughs*
>> Hardy

Smug, behind glass, we watch the passengers,
like cattle breaking, disembark.
One life, one marriage later I watched Gregorias stride
across the tarmac at Piarco, that familiar lope
that melancholy hunter's stride
seemed broken, part of the herd.
                    Something inside
me broke subtly, like a vein. I saw him grope
desperately, vaguely for his friend,
for something which a life's bewilderment could claim
as stable. I shouted, "Apilo!"
Panic and wonder struggled for the grin.

"O the years, O . . ."
                    The highway canes unrolled in
silence past the car glass, like glass
the years divided. We fished for the right level, shrill,
hysterical, until, when it subsided,
a cautionary silence glazed each word.
Was he as broken down as I had heard,

driven deep in debt,
unable to hold down a job, painting so badly
that those who swore his genius vindicated
everything once, now saw it as a promise never kept?
Viciously, near tears, I wished him dead.

I wished him a spiteful martyrdom, in revenge
for their contempt, their tiring laughter.
After I told him, he laughed and said, "I tried it once."

"One morning I lay helplessly in bed,
everything drained, gone. The children crying.
I couldn't take any more. I had dreamed of dying.
I sent for Peggy, you remember her?
She's in the States now. Anyhow,
I sent her to the bathroom for a blade . . .
When she had brought it, I asked her to go.
I lay there with the razor-blade in my hand . . .
I tried to cut my wrist . . . I don't know why
I stopped. I wanted very, very much to die . . .
Only some nights before, I had had a dream . . .
I dreamt . . ."
                              And what use what he dreamt?
"We lived in a society which denied itself heroes"
(Naipaul), poor scarred carapace
shining from those abrasions it has weathered,
wearing his own humility like a climate,
a man exhausted, racked by his own strength,
Gregorias, I saw, had entered life.

They shine, they shine,
such men. After the vision

of their own self-exhaustion bores them,
till, slowly unsurprised at their own greatness,
needing neither martyrdom nor magnificence,
"I see, I see," is what Gregorias cried,
living within that moment where he died.

Re-reading Pasternak's *Safe Conduct*
as always again when life
startles under the lamplight,
I saw him brutally as Mayakovsky,
nostalgia, contempt raged for his death,
and the old choir of frogs,
those spinsterish, crackling cicadas.
Yet, even in such books
the element has burnt out,
honour and revelation are
a votive flame, and what's left
is too much like a wreath,
a smoky, abrupt recollection.
I write of a man whom life,
not death or memory, grants fame,
in my own pantheon, so, while
this fiery particle
thrives fiercely in another,
even if fuelled by liquour
to venerate the good,
honour the humbly great,
to render in "an irresponsible citizen"
the simple flame.

Too late, too late.

ii

The rain falls like knives
on the kitchen floor.
The sky's heavy drawer
was pulled out too suddenly.
The raw season is on us.

For days it has huddled on the kitchen sill,
tense, a smoke and orange kitten
flexing its haunches,
coiling its yellow scream
and now, it springs.
Nimble fingers of lightning
have picked the watershed,
the wires fling their beads.
Tears, like slow crystal beetles, crawl the pane.

On such days, when the postman's bicycle
whirrs drily like the locust
that brings rain, I dread my premonitions.
A grey spot, a waterdrop
blisters my hand.
A sodden letter thunders in my hand.
The insect gnaws steadily at its leaf,
an eaten letter crumbles in my hand,
as he once held my drawing to his face,
as though dusk were myopic, not his gaze.

"Harry has killed himself. He was found dead
in a house in the country. He was dead for two days."

132

iii

The fishermen, like thieves, shake out their silver,
the lithe knives wriggle on the drying sand.
They go about their work,
their chronicler has gone about his work.

At Garand, at Piaille, at L'Anse la Verdure,
the sky is grey as pewter, without meaning.
It thunders and the kitten scuttles back
into the kitchen bin
of coal, its tines sheathing, unsheathing,
its yellow eyes the colour of fool's gold.

He had left this note.
No meaning, and no meaning.

All day, on the tin roofs
the rain berates the poverty of life,
all day the sunset bleeds like a cut wrist.

iv

Well, there you have your seasons, prodigy!
For instance, the autumnal fall of bodies,
deaths, like a comic, brutal repetition,
and in the Book of Hours, that seemed so far,
the light and amber of another life,
there is a Reaper busy about his wheat,
one who stalks nearer, and will not look up
from the scythe's swish in the orange evening grass,

and the fly at the font of your ear
sings, Hurry, hurry!
Never to set eyes on this page,
ah Harry, never to read our names,
like a stone blurred with tears I could not read
among the pilgrims, and the mooning child
staring from the window of the high studio.

Brown, balding, with a lacertilian
jut to his underlip,
with spectacles thick as a glass paperweight
and squat, blunt fingers,
waspish, austere, swift with asperities,
with a dimpled pot for a belly from the red clay of Piaille.
Eyes like the glint of sea-smoothed bottle glass,
his knee-high khaki stockings,
brown shoes lacquered even in desolation.

People entered his understanding
like a wayside country church,
they had built him themselves.
It was they who had smoothed the wall
of his clay-coloured forehead,
who made of his rotundity an earthy
useful object
holding the clear water of their simple troubles,
he who returned their tribal names
to the adze, mattock, midden and cookingpot.

A tang of white rum on the tongue of the mandolin,
a young bay, parting its mouth,
a heron silently named or a night-moth,
or the names of villages plaited into one map,

in the evocation of scrubbed back-yard smoke,
and he is a man no more
but the fervour and intelligence
of a whole country.

Leonce, Placide, Alcindor,
Dominic, from whose plane vowels were shorn
odorous as forest,
ask the charcoal-burner to look up
with his singed eyes,
ask the lip-cracked fisherman three miles at sea
with nothing between him and Dahomey's coast
to dip rain-water over his parched boards
for Monsieur Simmons, *pour* Msieu Harry Simmons,
let the husker on his pyramid of coconuts
rest on his tree.

Blow out the eyes in the unfinished portraits.

And the old woman who danced
with a spine like the "glory cedar,"
so lissome that her veins bulged evenly
upon the tightened drumskin of the earth,
her feet nimbler than the drummer's fingers,
let her sit in her corner and become evening
for a man the colour of her earth,
for a cracked claypot full of idle brushes,
and the tubes curl and harden,
except the red,
except the virulent red!

His island forest, open and enclose him
like a rare butterfly between its leaves.

chapter 21

Why?
You want to know why?
Go down to the shacks then,
like shattered staves
bound in old wire
at the hour when
the sun's wrist bleeds in
the basin of the sea,
and you will sense it,

or follow the path
of the caked piglet through
the sea-village's midden,
past the repeated
detonations of spray,
where the death-rattle
gargles in the shale,
and the crab,
like a letter, slides
into its crevice,
and you may understand this,

smell the late, ineradicable reek
of stale rags like rivers
at daybreak, or the dark corner

of the salt-caked shop where the cod-
barrel smells of old women,
and you can start then,

to know how the vise
of horizon tightens
the throat, when the first sulphur star
catches the hum
of insects round the gas lantern
like flies round a sore.
No more? Then hang round the lobby
of the one cinema too early

in the hour between two illusions
where you startle at the chuckle
of water under the shallop
of the old schooner basin,
or else it is still under all
the frighteningly formal
marches of banana groves,
the smell from the armpits of cocoa,

from the dead, open mouths
of husked nuts
on the long beach at twilight,
old mouths filled with water,
or else with no more to say.

ii

So you have ceased to ask yourself,
nor do these things ask you,
for the bush too is an answer

without a question,
as the sea is a question, chafing,
impatient for answers,
and we are the same.
They do not ask us, master,
do you accept this?
A nature reduced to the service
of praising or humbling men,
there is a yes without a question,
there is assent founded on ignorance,
in the mangroves plunged to the wrist, repeating
the mangroves plunging to the wrist,
there are spaces
wider than conscience.

Yet, when I continue to see
the young deaths of others,
even of lean old men, perpetually young,
when the alphabet I learnt as a child
will not keep its order,
see the young wife, self-slain
like scentful clove in the earth,
a skin the colour of cinnamon,
there is something which balances,
I see him bent under the weight of the morning,
against its shafts,
devout, angelical,
the easel rifling his shoulder,
the master of Gregorias and myself,
I see him standing over the bleached roofs
of the salt-streaked villages,
each steeple pricked
by its own wooden star.

I who dressed too early for the funeral of this life,
who saw them all, as pilgrims of the night.

iii

And do I still love her, as I love you?
I have loved all women who have evolved from her,
fired by two marriages
to have her gold ring true.
And on that hill, that evening,
when the deep valley grew blue with forgetting,
why did I weep,
why did I kneel,
whom did I thank?
I knelt because I was my mother,
I was the well of the world,
I wore the stars on my skin,
I endured no reflections,
my sign was water,
tears and the sea,
my sign was Janus,
I saw with twin heads,
and everything I say is contradicted.

I was fluent as water,
I would escape
with the linear elation of an eel,
a vase of water in its vase of clay,
my clear tongue licked the freshness of the earth,
and when I leapt from that shelf
of rock, an abounding bolt of lace,
I leapt for the pride of that race
at Sauteurs! An urge more than mine,

so, see them as heroes or as the Gadarene swine,
let it be written, I shared, I shared,
I was struck like rock, and I opened
to His gift!
I laughed at my death-gasp in the rattle
of the sea-shoal.
You want to see my medals? Ask the stars.
You want to hear my history? Ask the sea.
And you, master and friend,
forgive me!
Forgive me, if this sketch should ever thrive,
or profit from your gentle, generous spirit.
When I began this work, you were alive,
and with one stroke, you have completed it!

O simultaneous stroke of chord and light,
O tightened nerves to which the soul vibrates,
some flash of lime-green water, edged with white—
"I have swallowed all my hates."

      iv

For I have married one whose darkness is a tree,
bayed in whose arms I bring my stifled howl,
love and forgive me!
Who holds my fears at dusk like birds which take
the lost or moonlit colour of her leaves,
in whom our children
and the children of friends settle
simply, like rhymes,
in whose side, in the grim times
when I cannot see light for the deep leaves,
sharing her depth, the whole lee ocean grieves.

chapter 22

Miasma, acedia, the enervations of damp,
as the teeth of the mould gnaw, greening the carious stump
of the beaten, corrugated silver of the marsh light,
where the red heron hides, without a secret,
as the cordage of mangrove tightens
bland water to bland sky
heavy and sodden as canvas,
where the pirogue foundered with its caved-in stomach
(a hulk, trying hard to look like
a paleolithic, half-gnawed memory of pre-history)
as the too green acid grasses set the salt teeth on edge,
acids and russets and water-coloured water,
let the historian go mad there
from thirst. Slowly the water rat takes up its reed pen
and scribbles. Leisurely, the egret
on the mud tablet stamps its hieroglyph.

The explorer stumbles out of the bush crying out for myth.
The tired slave vomits his past.
The Mediterranean accountant, with the nose of the water rat,
ideograph of the egret's foot,
calculates his tables,
his eyes reddening like evening in the glare of the brass lamp;
the Chinese grocer's smile is leaden with boredom:
so many lbs. of cod,

              so many bales of biscuits,
on spiked shop paper,
the mummified odour of onions,
spikenard, and old Pharaohs peeling like onionskin
to the archaeologist's finger—all that
is the muse of history. Potsherds,
and the crusted amphora of cutthroats.

Like old leather,
tannic, stinking, peeling in a self-contemptuous
curl away from itself,
the yellowing poems, the spiked brown paper,
the myth of the golden Carib,
like a worn-out film,
the lyrical arrow in the writhing Arawak maiden
broken under the leaf-light.
                              The astigmatic geologist
stoops, with the crouch of the heron,
deciphering—not a sign.
All of the epics are blown away with the leaves,
blown with the careful calculations on brown paper;
these were the only epics: the leaves.

No horsemen here, no cuirasses
crashing, no fork-bearded Castilians,
only the narrow, silvery creeks of sadness
like the snail's trail,
only the historian deciphering, in invisible ink,
its patient slime,
no cataracts abounding down gorges
like bolts of lace,
while the lizards are taking a million years to change,
and the lopped head of the coconut rolls to gasp on the sand,

its mouth open at the very moment
of forgetting its name.

That child who sets his half-shell afloat
in the brown creek that is Rampanalgas River—
my son first, then two daughters—
towards the roar of waters,
towards the Atlantic with a dead almond leaf for a sail,
with a twig for a mast,
was, like his father, this child,
a child without history, without knowledge of its pre-world,
only the knowledge of water runnelling rocks,
and the desperate whelk that grips the rock's outcrop
like a man whom the waves can never wash overboard;
that child who puts the shell's howl to his ear,
hears nothing, hears everything
that the historian cannot hear, the howls
of all the races that crossed the water,
the howls of grandfathers drowned
in that intricately swivelled Babel,
hears the fellaheen, the Madrasi, the Mandingo, the Ashanti,
yes, and hears also the echoing green fissures of Canton,
and thousands without longing for this other shore
by the mud tablets of the Indian Provinces,
robed ghostly white and brown, the twigs of uplifted hands,
of manacles, mantras, of a thousand kaddishes,
whorled, drilling into the shell,
see, in the evening light by the saffron, sacred Benares,
how they are lifting like herons,
robed ghostly white and brown,
and the crossing of water has erased their memories.
And the sea, which is always the same,
accepts them.

And the shore, which is always the same,
accepts them.

In the shallop of the shell,
in the round prayer,
in the palate of the conch,
in the dead sail of the almond leaf
are all of the voyages.

ii

And those who gild cruelty,
who read from the entrails of disembowelled Aztecs
the colors of Hispanic glory
greater than Greece,
greater than Rome,
than the purple of Christ's blood,
the golden excrement on barbarous altars
of their beaked and feathered king,
and the feasts of human flesh,
those who remain fascinated,
in attitudes of prayer,
by the festering roses made from their fathers' manacles,
or upraise their silver chalices flecked with vomit,
who see a golden, cruel, hawk-bright glory
in the conquistador's malarial eye,
crying, at least here
something happened—
they will absolve us, perhaps, if we begin again,
from what we have always known, nothing,
from that carnal slime of the garden,
from the incarnate subtlety of the snake,
from the Egyptian moment of the heron's foot

on the mud's entablature,
by this augury of ibises
flying at evening from the melting trees,
while the silver-hammered charger of the marsh light
brings towards us, again and again, in beaten scrolls,
nothing, then nothing,
and then nothing.

iii

Here, rest. Rest, heaven. Rest, hell.
Patchwork, sunfloor, seafloor of pebbles at Resthaven, Rampanalgas.
Sick of black angst.
Too many penitential histories passing
for poems. Avoid:
1857 Lucknow and Cawnpore.
The process of history machined through fact,
for the poet's cheap alcohol,
lines like the sugarcane factory's mechanization of myth
ground into rubbish.
1834 Slavery abolished.
A century later slavishly revived
for the nose of the water rat, for the literature of the factory,
in the masochistic veneration of
chains, and the broken rum jugs of cutthroats.
Exegesis, exegesis, writers
giving their own sons homework.

Ratoon, ratoon,
immigrant hordes downed soughing,
sickled by fever, *mal d'estomac,*
earth-eating slaves fitted with masks against despair,
not mental despondence but helminthiasis.

145

Pour la dernière fois, nommez! Nommez!

Abouberika Torre commonly called Joseph Samson.
Hammadi Torrouke commonly called Louis Modeste.
Mandingo sergeants offered Africa back,
the boring process of repatriation,
while to the indentured Indians
the plains of Caroni seemed like the Gangetic plain,
our fathers' bones. Which father?

Burned in the pyre of the sun.
On the ashpit of the sand.
Also you, Grandfather. Rest, heaven, rest, hell.
I sit in the roar of that sun
like a lotus yogi folded on his bed of coals,
my head is circled with a ring of fire.

iv

O sun, on that morning,
did I not mutter towards your
holy, repetitive resurrection, "Hare,
hare Krishna," and then, politely,
"Thank you, life"? Not
to enter the knowledge of God
but to know that His name
had lain too familiar on my tongue,
as this one would say "bread,"
or "sun," or "wine," I staggered,
shaken at my remorse, as one
would say "bride," or "bread,"
or "sun," or "wine," to believe—
and that you would rise again,

146

when I am not here, to catch
the air afire, that you need not
look for me, or need this prayer.

V

So, I shall repeat myself,
prayer, same prayer, towards fire, same fire,
as the sun repeats itself and the thundering waters

for what else is there
but books, books and the sea,
verandahs and the pages of the sea,
to write of the wind and the memory of wind-whipped hair
in the sun, the colour of fire?

I was eighteen then, now I am forty-one,
I have had a serpent for companion,
I was a heart full of knives,
but, my son, my sun,

holy is Rampanalgas and its high-circling hawks,
holy are the rusted, tortured, rust-caked, blind almond trees,
your great-grandfather's, and your father's torturing limbs,
holy the small, almond-leaf-shadowed bridge
by the small red shop, where everything smells of salt,
and holiest the break of the blue sea below the trees,
and the rock that takes blows on its back
and is more rock,
and the tireless hoarse anger of the waters
by which I can walk calm, a renewed, exhausted man,
balanced at its edge by the weight of two dear daughters.

vi

Holy were you, Margaret,
and holy our calm.
What can I do now

but sit in the sun to burn
with an ageing mirror that blinds,
combing, uncombing my hair—

escape? No, I am inured
only to the real, which
burns. Like the flesh

of my children afire.
Inured. Inward. As rock,
I wish, as the real

rock I make real,
to have burnt out desire,
lust, except for the sun

with her corona of fire.
Anna, I wanted to grow white-haired
as the wave, with a wrinkled

brown rock's face, salted,
seamed, an old poet,
facing the wind

and nothing, which is,
the loud world in his mind.

chapter 23

At the Malabar Hotel cottage
I would wake every morning surprised
by the framed yellow jungle of
the groyned mangroves meeting
the groyned mangroves repeating
their unbroken water-line.
Years. The island had not moved
from anchor.
                    Generations of waves,
generations of grass, like foam
petalled and perished in an instant.

I lolled in the shallows like an ageing hammerhead
afraid of my own shadow, hungering there.
When my foot struck sand, the sky rang,
as I inhaled, a million leaves drew inward.
I bent towards what I remembered,
all was inevitably shrunken,
it was I who first extended my hand
to nameless arthritic twigs,
and a bush would turn in the wind
with a toothless giggle, and
certain roots refused English.
But I was the one in awe.

This was a new pain,
I mean the mimosa's averring
"You mightn't remember me,"
like the scars of that scrofulous sea-grape
where Gregorias had crucified a canvas,
and there, still dancing like the old woman
was the glory, the *gloricidia*.
I would not call up Anna.
I would not visit his grave.

ii

They had not changed, they knew only
the autumnal hint of hotel rooms
the sea's engine of air-conditioners,
and the waitress in national costume
and the horsemen galloping past the single wave
across the line of Martinique, the horse or *la mer*
out of Gauguin by the Tourist Board.
Hotel, hotel, hotel, hotel, hotel and a club: The Bitter End.
This is not bitter, it is harder
to be a prodigal than a stranger.

iii

I looked from old verandahs at
verandahs, sails, the eternal summer sea
like a book left open by an absent master.
And what if it's all gone,
the hill's cut away for more tarmac,
the groves all sawn,
and bungalows proliferate on the scarred, hacked hillside,

the magical lagoon drained
for the Higher Purchase plan,
and they've bulldozed and bowdlerised our Vigie,
our *ocelle insularum*, our Sirmio
for a pink and pastel NewTown where the shacks and huts stood
teetering and tough in unabashed unhope,
as twilight like amnesia blues the slope,
when over the untroubled ocean, the moon
will always swing its lantern
and evening fold the pages of the sea,
and peer like my lost reader silently
between the turning leaves
for the lost names
of Caribs, slaves and fishermen?

Forgive me, you folk,
who exercise a patience
subtler, stronger than the muscles
in the wave's wrist,
and you, sea, with the mouth
of that old gravekeeper
white-headed, lantern-jawed,
forgive our desertions, you islands
whose names dissolve like sugar
in a child's mouth. And you, Gregorias.
And you, Anna. Rest.

iv

But, ah Gregorias,
I christened you with that Greek name because
it echoes the blest thunders of the surf,

because you painted our first, primitive frescoes,
because it sounds explosive,
a black Greek's! A sun that stands back
from the fire of itself, not shamed, prizing
its shadow, watching it blaze!
You sometimes dance with that destructive frenzy
that made our years one fire.
Gregorias listen, lit,
we were the light of the world!
We were blest with a virginal, unpainted world
with Adam's task of giving things their names,
with the smooth white walls of clouds and villages
where you devised your inexhaustible,
impossible Renaissance,
brown cherubs of Giotto and Masaccio,
with the salt wind coming through the window,
smelling of turpentine, with nothing so old
that it could not be invented,
and set above it your crude wooden star,
its light compounded in that mortal glow:
Gregorias, Apilo!

April 1965–April 1972